D0246902

THE TIMES

ULTIMATE

SUPERCARS

Dedicated to my two little supercar experts, A.B. and K.A.

Times Books
An imprint of HarperCollins*Publishers*
1 London Bridge Street
London SE1 9GF
www.harpercollins.co.uk

First published by HarperCollins*Publishers* in 2014
This Times Books edition published in 2015

10 9 8 7 6 5 4 3 2 1

A catalogue record for this book is available from the British Library

ISBN 978-0-00-795005-8

THE TIMES

ULTIMATE SUPERCARS

MARTIN ROACH

INTRODUCTION BY

DAVID COULTHARD

TIMES BOOKS

LONDON

CONTENTS

Introduction by David Coulthard 6
Author's Note 10

A Prehistory of Supercars 14
GAME CHANGER *1953 Mercedes-Benz 300 SL 'Gullwing'* 24
Also in the 1950s 36

The 1960s 38
GAME CHANGER *1963 Porsche 911* 46
GAME CHANGER *1966 Lamborghini Miura* 56
Also in the 1960s 66

Muscle or Super? 72

The 1970s 84
GAME CHANGER *1974 Lamborghini Countach* 90
Also in the 1970s 102

The 1980s 106
GAME CHANGER *1986 Porsche 959* 118
GAME CHANGER *1987 Ferrari F40* 128
Also in the 1980s 138

The 1990s 142
GAME CHANGER *1992 McLaren F1* 150
GAME CHANGER *1999 Pagani Zonda* 166
Also in the 1990s 174

The 2000s and Onwards 178
GAME CHANGER *2005 Bugatti Veyron* 188
Also in the 2000s and Onwards 214
GAME CHANGER *Hybrids and the Future of Supercars* 226

Conclusion 242
Afterword 246
Index 250
Quick Reference Glossary 253
Photo Credits 254
Author's Acknowledgements 256

AMG

Introduction by David Coulthard MBE

Mobility is a huge part of the modern world. One of the first expressions of independence for anyone, as a child, is getting a bicycle and learning to ride. That moment, when your mum or dad takes their hands off the back of the seat and you are cycling on your own, is a pivotal one for us all, because from that point you can propel yourself.

The logical extension of that is moving on to four wheels, so getting to 17, passing your driving test and buying your first car is a big aspiration. You might not go out and get a supercar as your first vehicle, but that ultimate dream is often there.

Of course, long before you can go anywhere near an accelerator pedal yourself, supercars might play a big part in your life. When I was a boy, I had a Lamborghini poster on my bedroom wall, as well as some pictures of racing cars (I was a big fan of Alain Prost). It was the typical lad's room and, despite being strict, my mother respected the fact that it was my domain. My father was pretty much a Mercedes man and we tended to have family saloons, no supercars as such, but cars have always been a part of what my family was about.

Obviously, because of my racing career, I have been driving vehicles from an early age. In terms of road cars, in the early days after my driving test I had a Renault 5 that I loved and, admittedly, occasionally drove quite hard! In a sense I am not your typical supercar fan because, at the age of 19, I went straight from Scotland to driving a McLaren V12 Formula 1 car. That machine kind of takes the notion of a supercar being powerful and blows it out of the water, I guess, but that didn't stop me admiring supercars all these years.

I live in Monaco and I cycle around here all the time, so I obviously see a lot of supercars on the streets around town. I absolutely love looking at them. They are beautiful creations and I can see why people spend so much money on them. The majority of people are touched more by how things look than by how they perform. Supercars have always been desirable, an admired and accepted blend of art and functionality. They are beautiful works of art. Someone else might buy a painting and look at that, admire the skill and creativity of the artist. A supercar is no different, except that it has function as well as form.

You don't *need* to buy a supercar, of course. You can buy a budget car that will take you to the same place, albeit more slowly and in less style than a million-pound supercar. You can also spend thousands of pounds on a bespoke home stereo system, or you could just stick your iPod in a dock and get the same songs played in your house to a very good standard. In that sense, why buy anything that is more expensive than what you might practically need? That's not the point – everyone has their passion and if supercars are your passion, and you have the means to buy them, then that is your prerogative. You don't need to justify a supercar.

People wonder why you'd spend so much money on a car that often sits under a dust sheet. That to me is a pointless question. It is the individual's right to live their particular dream. The person who questions the point of supercars will perhaps be more into steam locomotives or fly fishing, neither of which are for me, but we are all different.

Supercars are also about brands, and about how owners and fans feel when they associate themselves with other people – are you a flamboyant Lamborghini type or a stylish Ferrari man? Or maybe McLaren's technological excellence appeals more to your precise character? Every car marque has its own expression, and supercars are an extreme way of representing brand values.

Supercars also affect us all in the same way that Formula 1 technology impacts on our lives. There are so many crossover synergies and drop-downs that naturally come with high-level technology. If you engineer something to go to the Moon, then finding something that can go to 35,000 feet is relatively straightforward by comparison. If you are engineering something that can do 200mph, and as part of your group you are also designing a family run-around, your understanding of extreme engineering naturally filters down to affordable engineering. So, supercars are a great example of the highest level of road cars affecting everyday cars.

Supercars do seem to be an almost universal fascination for millions of people around the world, and that alone is sufficient justification for their existence. In this ever-changing world, where there are ever more green requirements for manufacturers to adhere to, supercars are growing more popular and commercially stronger than ever. This is not because people are rebelling against legislation and regulation, but because more people have the means to enjoy that refined mobility and complex engineering. Supercars are now as culturally popular as they have ever been. So I totally understand people's enjoyment of supercars.

If I decided to go out and buy a supercar today I'd have to buy several, so I'd want a McLaren F1, a Lamborghini and a Gullwing. The Ferrari 458 is lovely, too. I couldn't just pick one, because I can see something wonderful in all these amazing cars.

Supercars are mobile works of art, the ultimate expression of engineering, performance and style. They are highly subjective, too, and so what Martin tried to do in this book is to recount the history of these amazing machines while also highlighting the key game changers – as well as many other incredible examples of important supercars – in a way that reflects this subjectivity. He has used his own perspective to emphasise the personal nature of these engineering feats. Maybe reading this will encourage you to buy a supercar, or perhaps just a supercar poster or model. Either way, your world and all of our lives, too, are better off for having supercars in them.

David Coulthard MBE, Monaco, April 2014

Author's Note

When I was a kid, I had a poster of a red Lamborghini Countach on my wall. I had seen a Countach on a school trip to London and my mind was completely blown away by this spaceship on wheels, this creation, this other-worldly machine that seemed to have landed from another planet. That weekend I went to a shop called Athena with my pocket money and bought that Countach poster, as well as a small, white, die-cast model of the same car.

I have been fascinated by supercars ever since, much to the annoyance of my wife and to the detriment of my bank account, which is repeatedly depleted by purchases of 'essential' die-cast models to add to my collection. Throughout my childhood and into my adulthood that die-cast collection grew, and so did my fascination with supercars, and this has ultimately led me to write this book.

Before we embark on this subjective journey through the supercar world, I should explain the criteria I've used to decide what qualifies as a 'supercar'. For certain, a supercar has to look sensational. Also, its performance needs to be either ground-breaking, in some capacity, or at least ridiculously impressive in terms of power and speed. Even today, when most supercars' top speeds are impossible to reach on public roads – for example, the Bugatti Veyron Super Sport can go nearly 200mph faster than the UK speed limit – for some reason we still hanker after these headline figures. For that reason, many of the cars in this book will have been the fastest in the world at the time of their launch, although not all of them. Exclusivity is also key; with low production numbers and, of course, a high price to match. The noise these cars make is part of the decision, too. But there is also a final, intangible criterion – for want of a better word, an 'X factor'; some emotional, subjective feeling that tells you a certain car is very special. A supercar is something that you climb into to drive for the sake of it, almost regardless of where you are going. A supercar is an *event*.

All of these elements help to define what I feel qualifies as a supercar. I have not covered modified or concept cars, nor (generally) cars that use 'donor' vehicles. More generally, I have looked only at the modern car, meaning those produced in the 1950s onwards (I will explain why shortly). I have organised the book into decades, with each car dated from its production. Within the selection of cars, I have included ten so-called 'Game Changers', vehicles that in my opinion are so significant they deserve their own feature chapter. These are cars that were so revolutionary – for a number of reasons, which will be explained – that they changed the supercar game beyond recognition. Cars so startlingly original, they made their rival manufacturers go into work the next morning and call an emergency meeting. Back-to-the-drawing-board levels of panic. There are, of course, many fabulous supercars that really did create a storm when they were launched, but my group of game changers is a little more select.

What this book will not list is extensive technical details, so, you will not find a lengthy analysis of the type of alloy used in a certain wheel, or the specific width of a piston rod, and so on. I have also avoided any 'test drive' reports, because these are widely available in the huge number of amazing car magazines and websites, whose experts deliver minutely detailed driving analyses of supercars every week.

I have instead tried to delve into the back stories of the cars, the people behind them, and the *personalities* of these amazing machines. Supercars are incredible technical feats, but the most successful examples are also those cars that make us *feel* special, whether by driving, owning or simply looking at them. Each one of us has an emotional connection with our favourite supercars: a relationship. To get to the root of that relationship, you need to know the story of each car.

So, see which cars you like best, which ones you think are game changers, and which ones you might have included in your own Top Ten, too. No doubt you will disagree with some of my choices, and hopefully the book will spark some debate for you. Whether you are a boy who loves supercars or a 'bigger boy' who enjoys them just the same, this book is for you.

As I write this, I have a chipped and rather old 1:43 scale model of a Lamborghini Countach – now used as a paperweight – on my desk. Somewhere in a box in the attic, I still have my dog-eared poster, too.

PREVIOUS PAGE ***The Lamborghini Countach is considered by many to be the definitive supercar and was the childhood dream car of millions of kids around the world.***

RIGHT ***The 2005 launch of the Bugatti Veyron reignited a long-dormant marque and in so doing redefined almost every parameter and benchmark for a modern supercar.***

A Prehistory of Supercars

LEFT ***Benz's first-ever car, the Motorwagen, had many elements that would later be found on supercars – including an accelerator system, a spark plug and a clutch.***

This book focuses on what can be loosely termed the 'modern supercar' – namely, certain vehicles from the post-war period, specifically the 1950s onwards. However, by the time of the first of my ten game changers in this book – the 1954 Mercedes-Benz Gullwing – the car as an invention had been around for almost 70 years. So why am I suggesting that in the decades before this modern era the supercar as we know it did not essentially exist?

Well, of course, this notion is nonsense in some ways. If a supercar is defined by being technologically advanced, quicker than its rivals, a 'head turner' in the street and capable of altering the automotive world overnight, then the very first commercially available car, the Benz Motorwagen from 1886, is surely also the first ever supercar. In that year, Carl Benz had patented his three-wheeled, single-cylinder car with a four-stroke internal combustion engine running on coal gas. However, it was his daring wife Bertha who was brave enough to take the ingenious machine out on the open road, thus making the first ever car journey. Bertha was convinced of her husband's idea, while he had a cautious reluctance to test the machine on real roads – Germany's Kaiser loved horses and had said replacing them was unpatriotic, while the Church had even declared the horseless carriage to be the work of the devil! Bertha was undeterred, however, and decided to take a secretive, 60-mile test trip to her mother's house in Pforzheim. In the process, she stopped to make a minor spring repair with her garter belt, and also to clean a blocked fuel line with a hat pin. She even called in at a shoemaker's to get the brake pads relined with leather. Thus, all at once, Bertha Benz became an automotive legend: the first car thief, the greatest car marketeer the world had ever seen and, arguably, the driver of the first ever supercar.

After that momentous first journey, it wasn't long before the human desire to push boundaries took over. While it was left to innovators such as Henry Ford to work out how to make cars cheaper, there was always a group of extreme individuals who were figuring out how to go *faster*.

Of course, once you have people competing to be the fastest, you have a race. History books tell us that the first ever true motor race took place in 1895 (there had been an earlier event driving from Paris to Rouen, but that was focused on reliability rather than speed). With the anniversary of the first decade of motoring in mind, a race was organised to go from Paris to Bordeaux and back: a distance of no less than 723 miles. A gentleman called Emile Levassor arrived first, in a single-cylinder car boasting four brake horsepower and averaging a speed of 14.9mph. His win took 48 hours, 48 minutes and he drove the entire race alone. (Out of twenty-two entrants, a clockwork car started and among the eight finishers was a steam car.) Importantly, the race confirmed the internal combustion engine as the premier method for car propulsion. Within a few years, the Royal Automobile Club of Great Britain was organising an incredible 1,000-mile endurance race.

These formative cars might have been slow by modern standards but the technological advances behind them were moving at lightning speed. In

BELOW ***In December 1900, the 35bhp Mercedes became the first vehicle to bear the name Mercedes. It was named after Mercedes Jellinek, the 11-year-old daughter of businessman and automobile enthusiast Emil Jellinek. Many people consider the first Mercedes to be not only the first modern car, but also the first real supercar. With its low centre of gravity and lightweight, low-mounted, high-performance engine, it marked a final break from the 'motorised coach' style of design that had dominated until then. This innovative vehicle caused a sensation; in particular, in the wake of its triumphs at Nice Race Week in March 1901.***

ABOVE ***The Bentley Boys were a group of wealthy men from the upper classes, who raced hard and played hard. They included among their lavish ranks an aviator, a pearl fisherman, a diamond magnate, a steeplechaser and various financiers, whose antics on and off the race track kept the company's profile high.***

1896, things became even more 'super' when the infamous Red Flag Law was repealed. In the second half of the 19th century, some scientists claimed that if the human body went faster than a horse could gallop, then death would almost certainly result. With this as well as pedestrian safety in mind, legislation had been introduced decreeing cars so fast and dangerous that every motor vehicle was required to have a man walking in front of it waving a red flag, and to keep to speeds of no more than 2mph in towns. With this restriction now removed, and a speed limit of 12mph established, the race to create the modern-day supercar had truly started.

Within two years, the first-ever world speed record was set by Frenchman Gaston de Chasseloup-Laubat. He achieved this in an electric car made by manufacturer Jeantaud, which reached 39.24mph. In the late 1800s, a car reaching 50mph as a top speed was considered breathtakingly fast, yet within ten years this benchmark was upped to 100mph; and by 1927, it was over 200mph. Early car marques such as Panhard, Darracq and Brouhot were the ones to watch in the late 19th and early 20th centuries. However, the onset of the First World War blighted a lot of industrial manfacturing, as resources were diverted to the war effort.

After the war, the 1920s saw the start of the golden era of so-called 'gentlemen racers': wealthy and innovative engineers such as Ferdinand Porsche, Ettore Bugatti and Enzo Ferrari, who would create racing cars and then personally race them on tracks around Europe. If a part didn't work on a race day, they would repair it during the week and then race the new version a few days later. They would often drive the cars to the track

RIGHT ***The Blower was a 4.5-litre Bentley made in 1927, which had a massive supercharger strapped, quite literally, to the front of the car. This resulted in a massive power boost that made the car unreliable but brutally fast. It won a number of top-speed competitions. Today, it is regarded as the definitive pre-war Bentley, and examples can fetch in excess of £2 million ($3.4 million). In the very early James Bond novels (less so in the films), 007's car of choice was a Bentley Blower.***

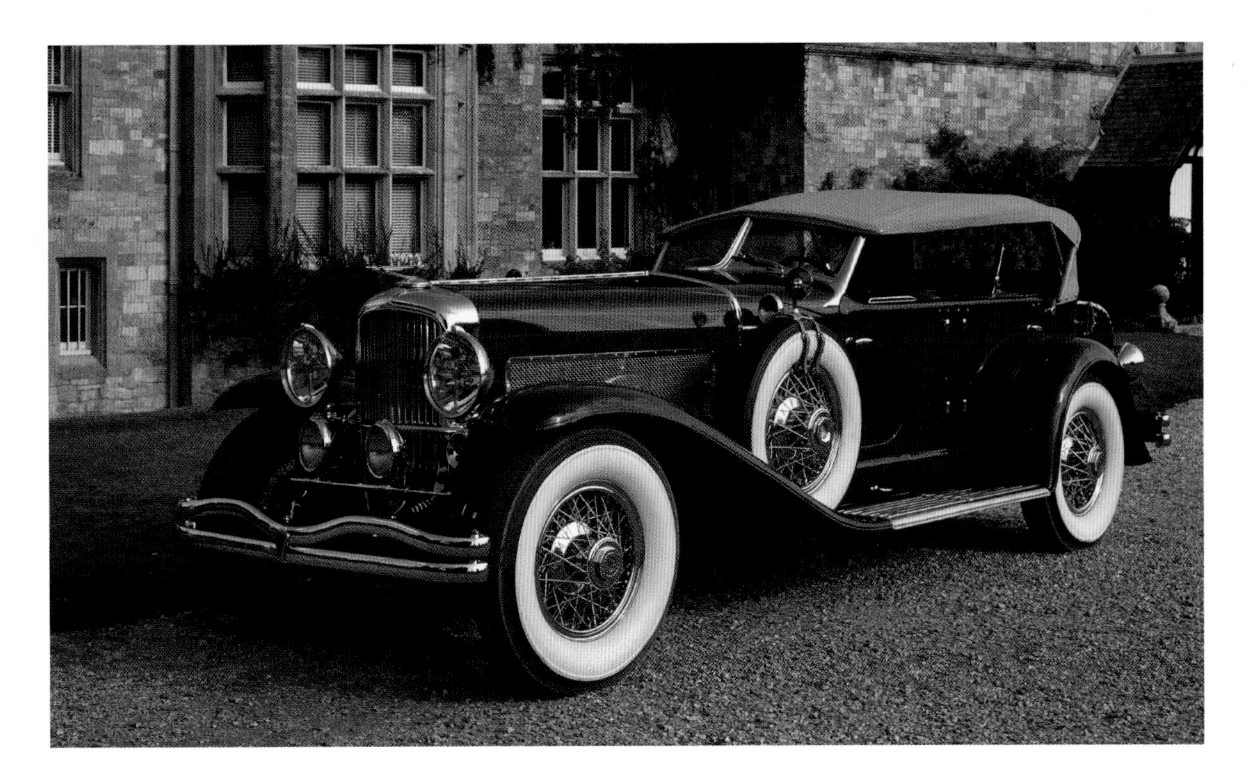

ABOVE ***In the 1920s and 1930s, many car buyers opted for ultra-luxury rather than stripped-back speed. For example, the iconic Duesenberg cars were offered as rolling chassis to which you applied your bodywork of choice, hand-made by a coachbuilder. These bodies were exorbitantly expensive and used only the very finest technology and materials. A Duesenberg chassis was 19 times more expensive than an entire Ford Model T – hence, the famous American phrase, 'It's a Duesie', used to describe anything that is the very best.***

on public roads, simply take off the lights and then go racing. After the chequered flag, they would drink expensive spirits and smoke rare cigars before popping the lights back on and heading home. Famous battles at races such as Le Mans, Mille Miglia, Targa Florio and the TT became a breeding ground for fast cars. The 1920s also marked the beginning of race technology filtering down into road cars. For example, front-wheel drive, double-overhead camshafts and multiple valves were all first proven in racing cars during this period.

A few of these early cars are worthy of note in order to colour this prehistory of supercars. For example, the Bentley Blower was a massive car born of an unashamed addiction to going fast. Another noteworthy early contributor to supercar prehistory is the elegant Bugatti Type 35. Only 200 of this amazing little lightweight racer were built, complete with an eight-cylinder, two-litre engine that dominated racing in the 1920s. Later, in the 1930s, the Type 35 had the world's first alloy wheels, and – incredibly – this combination of lightweight ethos and classic engine bagged in excess of 2,000 career race wins.

Similarly important cars include the Mercedes SSK (crowned by Mercedes as 'the world's first supercar'), the Bugatti Type 57, the Chrysler 300, Stutz Beacats, Duesenberg SJs, the Vauxhall 30/98 and the Alfa Romeo 8C Tipo B Monoposto. All of them used innovative technology. The Alfa Romeo, for example, used lightweight aluminium, inspired by the aviation industry. This endowed it with an amazing power-to-weight ratio, a latter-day essential for the modern supercar.

Economic factors again restricted the explosion of car technology in the 1930s, when the the Great Depression sank the world into a deep financial crisis for much of the decade. Racing, however, continued to prosper, with the Italians doing well, although many British and French marques struggled; then the German government began to officially subsidise and support racing. This brought huge investment and massive success for cars such as Auto Unions and the Mercedes W series of racers. Race drivers were now big celebrities, and speed was being celebrated as man conquering nature in a brave new world. The 1930s saw many sports car models derived from racing cars, such as the Alfa Romeo 8C, Aston Martin Mk II and the Jaguar SS100. In terms of 'supercar' looks, there was no shortage of striking shapes either – the Pierce Silver Arrow was a notable example. The 1947 Cisitalia 202 was a truly stunning car, whose amazing curves would pre-date even the beautiful Jaguar E-Type by many years; very few were built but so seductive was its silhouette that the New York Museum of Modern Art added one to its collection.

Then, just as the signs of long-awaited economic recovery were beginning to be felt by motor manufacturers, the Second World War began. Once more, industrial energy, money and innovation were focused on the war effort. Another period of stasis had arrived.

In the post-war era, expensive sports cars came to be seen – by the less wealthy majority – as selfish and self-indulgent objects of extravagance in a world still trying to pick itself up from the horrors of war. Despite this, among the world's monied homes there seemed to be an enduring demand for faster, sleeker cars. Not long after the war ended in 1945, there were encouraging signs that car manufacturers were back into the business of going fast. Although Britain was struggling under rationing, expensive fuel prices and a weakened economy, America was powering ahead. In response, many British sports car manufacturers tried hard to export their

BELOW ***In 1930, Italian Count Trossi created a one-off version of the Mercedes Benz SSK supercar featuring a custom-built roadster body. This SSK, a supercharged 7.1-litre 2-seater, was the fastest car in the world on its launch in 1928. The car's agility won it many hillclimb races, including both the German Grand Prix and Mille Miglia in 1931.***

cars to the USA to capitalise on the strong economy. Cars such as the gorgeous Jaguar XK120 (the fastest car in the world on its launch) or the luxurious Aston Martin DB4 were quintessentially British and sold reasonably well overseas.

Destructive though it is, war can often be the mother of invention and the motor industry made great leaps forward during the 1940s. For example, the shortage of steel due to the war effort forced manufacturers to design cars with bodies constructed from lighter materials, leading to greater speed and agility. The 1946 J1 by Allard is just one of many examples of super-quick 1940s cars, some lightweight variants of which were capable of topping out at speeds over 100mph. By 1948, the brilliant Jaguar XK120 could reach over 120mph (hence the name). There followed a period of Jaguar Le Mans dominance; first with the C Type and then with the D Type scooping a hatful of trophies. Also launched in 1948 was the dainty Porsche 356; a precursor to that marque's legendary 911, but not yet powerful enough to qualify as an early supercar. And, of course, there was the 1949 Ferrari 166 MM Barchetta, which after the 125 Sport was one of the marque's first purpose-built, road-going sports cars, a 2-litre V12 that was also raced and which scored back-to-back victories at Mille Miglia in 1949 and 1950. Was this the foundation stone of Ferrari's future?

The next, crucial stage in the prehistory of supercars came in the 1950s (and to an even greater extent the 1960s) when motor racing reached new heights of popularity. In many ways, the post-war period was distinguished by the symbiotic relationship between racing cars and road vehicles. The old adage of 'win on Sunday, sell on Monday' was never more true than during this era, with marques such as Jaguar and Ford pouring huge sums of money into racing, in the hope of enjoying the profitable filter-down effect of boosted sales of their road-going cars. Despite having the odds stacked

BELOW ***The Bugatti Type 35. Its later cousin, the Bugatti Type 43, had an engine taken straight from the Grand Prix-winning Type 35.***

against it, British motorsport continued to enjoy success, and it was the racing genius of certain British innovators that would later alter the face of supercar history forever.

During the 1950s, it was the vogue to turn front-engined race cars into road-going versions: thus we were introduced to examples such as the Ferrari 375MM in 1953, the Ferrari 250GT and the fateful Porsche 550/500RS, in which actor James Dean would crash to his death. (Dean had owned the car for just nine days and had christened his pride and joy the 'Little B*****d'.)

Although the 1960s is often seen as the decade in which supercars arrived in earnest, there are also several noteworthy cars from the 1950s. Europe and Britain were far more conservative, at least in terms of styling (there was a big demand for modest, frugal cars), which created a generation of refined sports cars. Meanwhile, American cars experimented with ever-more extravagant fins and space-age styling, as well as a smattering of early muscle cars. Bodywork and aerodynamically concious designs meant the cars were getting sleeker by the year. Change was afoot. In 1956, Ferrari launched a series of cars known as 'superfasts' – considered by many to be forebears of the modern supercar. Others look to the start of that brand's series production cars as more deserving of that title. Americans might hold up the early Chryslers, or a Corvette. For the purposes of this book, however, the first 'game-changing' supercar in question came from the same German manufacturer as Benz's 1886 Motorwagen. When their latest car arrived in 1954, the 300 SL – better known as the 'Gullwing' – it looked quite simply as if it came from another planet. The modern supercar race was on…

ABOVE ***In 1902, the improved 40bhp Mercedes-Simplex succeeded the 35bhp Mercedes, which had been not only the first car to carry the name Mercedes, but was also in many ways the first modern automobile. It was also arguably the first 'real' supercar. Fast-forward five decades and Mercedes had something even more remarkable lying in wait…***

GAME CHANGER

1954 Mercedes-Benz 300 SL 'Gullwing'

I AM STANDING IN THE POURING RAIN at the side of an old race track in Surrey. It is freezing cold and I have just been sitting, gridlocked, in a motorway traffic jam for over an hour. I haven't eaten, I'm tired and I'm soaking wet, but I don't care. In fact, I feel like I have won the lottery. Why? Because I am standing next to a 1954 Mercedes-Benz 'Gullwing' 300 SL. This book's first game changer.

First up, a little rain-soaked context: many histories of supercars take 1966 to be their Year Zero, with the advent of the magnificent, mid-engined Lamborghini Miura. Using the most commonly accepted criteria – that a

ABOVE ***The Mercedes-Benz 300 SL Gullwing – the grandaddy of all supercars.***

mid-engine layout offers the perfect combination of balance, weight distribution and a low centre of gravity – then the Miura is indeed the first supercar (more on that later). However, I want to draw your attention back a decade to the stunning, front-engined car that I am standing next to in the rain. Okay, it's not mid-engined but it is surely a supercar, if not the grandaddy of all supercars. The Mercedes 300 SL was the fastest car in the world on its launch, capable of reaching 160mph during an era when 100mph was the norm, and with looks that were simply staggering.

The car was the brainchild of Mercedes' chief race engineer Rudolf Uhlenhaut. In the early-to-mid-1950s, Mercedes were dominating on the race track and in some ways the 300 SL was a road-going version of their amazingly successful Silver Arrows racing cars. The Gullwing's direct racing predecessor won the 24 Hours Du Mans in 1952, as well as the Carrera Panamericana endurance rally in its debut season, so the racing pedigree of the proposed new Mercedes was high. Those inside the automotive industry knew that a road-going version of this successful racer would be quite some package if Mercedes could pull it off.

Uhlenhaut was asked to build a new racing car from the bare bones of the luxurious and highly regarded 300 Sedan – in post-war Germany, the finances were simply not available to develop a car from scratch. Added to that, the factories of Daimler-Benz had been extensively bombed during the war, razing the majority of their production facilities to the ground. So, the car manufacturer was literally trying to rise from the ashes. In 1951, Mercedes' management called a meeting to discuss the design of a radical new sports car. Remarkably, the time from that initial meeting to the completion of the first 300 SL chassis would be just five months. Uhlenhaut used the core of the 300 Sedan's engine, four-speed manual transmission, and its suspension system as the nucleus of this new design. However, in many other ways this would be a pioneering car.

Back in Surrey, after I had finished drooling over the 300 SL's rain-spattered shape, the first question that sprang to mind was, 'Why does it have those glorious gullwing doors?' From a creative perspective, the answer lies within a quote from the Mercedes Benz race team manager, Alfred Neubauer, who simply said, 'Nowhere is it written that a door must open sideways.' In fact, the doors were not designed simply to look good; they were actually an engineering necessity due to the innovative space-frame chassis underneath. This strong and lightweight skeleton of steel tubes was a very early use on a road car and presented a major challenge for the skilled fabricators at Mercedes. These tubes were wrapped around the sides of the car, where normal door openings would have been. Consequently, the door sills needed to be unusually high. The gullwing doors were a necessity, then, to allow access into the vehicle – a structural consequence of the space-frame, rather than just a design flourish. We should be thankful for that, although you might not agree if you need to repair one, as the space-frame is both extremely pricey to work on and prone to leaks.

The gullwing door design was actually changed three times before the production version was finalised. The first prototype had used a handle with

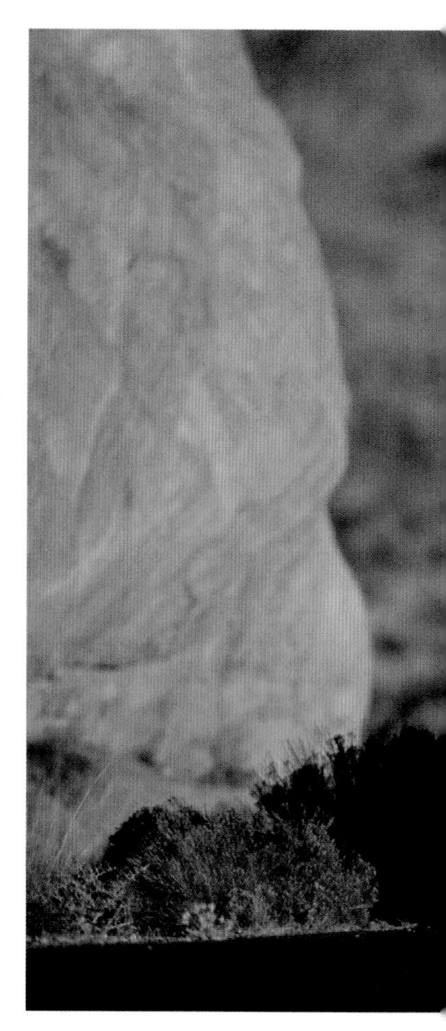

a hole for a finger grip, succeeded by a push-button, before the final design was implemented, which used a flush handle that pops out when depressed.

The 300 SL had two further notable elements, besides the space-frame and gullwing doors. The first was an independent four-wheel suspension, which improved the handling compared to many cars of the day. And, finally, the car was also the first road-going vehicle to successfully have direct fuel injection. Although fuel injection had been experimented with on car prototypes since the early 1930s, this was the very first example in actual production – an idea taken directly from aeronautical industry research. (Interestingly, one bulge in the 300 SL's hood was added to allow room for the fuel injection system, while the other bulge was included simply to make the car symmetrical.)

The car is mainly steel-bodied, with an aluminium bonnet, doors, rocker panels, firewall, floor, belly pans and boot lid. A small number of models were made with an all-aluminium skin. These rare versions now command huge premiums against the standard models, sometimes as high as five- or six-times the price. These special models can also be recognised by leather welts under their so-called 'eyebrows', fitted over the wheel arches to aid aerodynamics.

The stunning Sindelfingen design-bodied car was first seen in February 1954, but racing sports car prototypes had been unveiled back in 1952

BELOW ***The 300 SL was the first successful use of direct fuel injection in a production car. Two years previously, a Mercedes two-stroke-engined car had used the technology – without success.***

ABOVE **Due to the innovative space-frame chassis, the gullwings on the famous 300 SL were actually a design necessity, rather than a decorative flourish.**

(with two spare wheels in the tail, and a smaller cockpit turret top than the later road versions). Subverting most prototype-to-production car evolution standards, the eventual road-going 300 SL was actually more lean, daring and curvaceous than the prototype. That amazingly sleek body is actually made from 60 basic panels welded together.

The '300' refers to the 3-litre, flat-6 engine, which generated 220bhp (a racing camshaft option could increase this to 240bhp), while the SL stands for 'Super Leicht', meaning 'Super Light'. The engine is inclined at an angle of 50 degrees to the left to keep the centre of gravity as well as the height of the car down. A trial was planned using a supercharged racing version of the car – but this was abandoned, because the normally aspirated engine was already producing the maximum amount of horsepower that the rear axle could cope with.

Unlike future cars, such as the Porsche 959 and the Ferrari F40, which did not meet American regulations, the 300 SL was a vehicle targeted specifically at that market. American Mercedes dealer/distributor and former racing driver Max Hoffman felt a road-legal version of the marque's racing success story would be highly sought-after in the US, so Mercedes decided to build the car with America's wealthy post-war elite in mind. This is why the 300 SL was launched at the 1954 New York Auto Show, rather than in

Europe. America did not import exotic European cars in any volume at the time, but there was a growing population of affluent, expert purists who were looking to buy expensive continental cars. Hoffman knew his business well. So well, in fact, that he placed an order for 500 cars on the spot.

Oblivious to the rain, I was mulling over all of this history as I stood next to this magnificent silver example of the 300 SL – fittingly, a resident of the Mercedes World museum in Surrey. The museum is located next to Brooklands, the world's first purpose-built motor racing circuit, and it was a Mercedes that won the first race to take place there in 1907. Nowadays, the old circuit is complemented by a state-of-the-art modern museum and showroom facility, where brand-new Mercs sit next to priceless 19th century relics, as well as a shop, an AMG department and, rather delightfully, The Gullwing Bistro (which has normal restaurant doors, sadly, not gullwings).

I had been invited to see a 300 SL owned by Mercedes themselves, but first I had been out on track in the company's new flagship model – the staggering SLS AMG, which is classed by Mercedes as a 'spiritual successor' to the original Gullwing. I met the hugely amiable Mercedes driver, Ed, who walked me to a bright red SLS AMG, worth in the region of £175,000 ($295,000). I took that 570bhp monster out on the track and was allowed to fully rag it, losing the back end on the 'ice' pan and thoroughly enjoying the experience. It was an astonishing car and the driver aids were incredible, keeping the massive engine in hand and all the time making me feel like I was a much better driver than I actually am.

With the weather being so atrocious, I assumed that I would only be allowed to look at the 300 SL in some air-conditioned, pristine garage. However, after we had finished with the SLS AMG, Ed turned to me and said

RIGHT ***An original 1950s hand-drawn advert for the 300 SL.***

RIGHT While Mercedes had developed a fuel-injection system on a Gutbrod car from 1935, the Gullwing was the very first car to inject fuel directly into the cylinders. Mechanical rather than electrical, the fuel-injection system could be unreliable and required high maintenance. Some reports suggest certain elements were made from lambskin.

that he had 'warmed up' the original Gullwing and that we should head back to the centre. 'Warmed up' sounded promising (because you literally have to warm up the dry sump oil in a deep reservoir to protect this old engine before driving the car). I was delighted and very surprised when we pulled up and there she was, gleaming silver, the heavy drops of rain battering her 60-year-old paintwork. What a beautiful car. Looking at it, I understood what is often said about the 300 SL – that it 'looks fast standing still'.

I knew I wouldn't be allowed to drive the Gullwing but I didn't care; this was a privilege, regardless. I pulled the famous doors skywards and then slid into the deep-set maroon leather seats, each of which is stuffed with horsehair. Pulling the heavy gullwing down, Ed and I were both suddenly cocooned in a genuine slice of motoring history: a small cabin, lavishly wrapped in expensive-smelling leather, with a travel case at the back of our heads. The famously high sills become lovely armrests once you are inside. Every Gullwing instrument panel was painted the same colour as the external paintwork and this car was no exception. There were a few quirky features, too, such as the rear-view mirror being sited on the dashboard.

Ed chatted away about the car as we zipped around the track. He pointed out that the dials and switches have no labels, so when you first get in a Gullwing it is a process of trial and error to work out which one does what. (There was one switch that remained a mystery to Ed.) He also

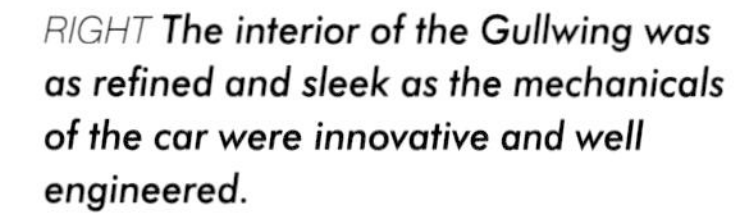
RIGHT ***The interior of the Gullwing was as refined and sleek as the mechanicals of the car were innovative and well engineered.***

explained the independent suspension, showing me how the car handled in corners and pointing out that when the large fuel tank was full, the car would handle completely differently.

All the time, the rain teemed down but I didn't care – the Gullwing was just so joyous. Then Ed said, 'We have a surprise for you. Would you like to drive?' I couldn't get out of the passenger seat quick enough. I virtually dragged Ed out of the driver's side and threw him on the track, before jumping in.

The steering wheel has a little lever that allows you to twist it forwards for easier access. You tilt the wheel forwards, slide down into the cabin and then put the wheel back into the driving position. The large two-spoke, *faux* ivory steering wheel itself was beautifully tactile, thin and slender. As I gingerly pulled the car away, I instantly noticed how heavy the clutch felt and for the first few corners I left the car in second gear, scared of losing control. No driver assists here. I had heard that the 300 SL's acceleration after 70mph is really impressive. I was not about to find out. The swing axle made hard-cornering a challenge, with plenty of oversteer, and I never felt fully confident, even in the low gears. The rather antiquated drum brakes seemed tough too but context is needed, however – these were the market-leading drum brakes at the time, in an era before disc brakes were universally adopted.

BELOW ***During one endurance race, the 300 SL racer hit a large donkey, ripping a big hole in the car's front bodywork. The car's high performance remained unaffected, however. Shortly afterwards, another driver hit a buzzard, shattering the windshield and showering him and his co-driver in glass shards. They stopped, bandaged their wounds, then continued with the race.***

Mercedes-Benz 300 SL

LAUNCHED

1954

POWER

The '300' refers to the 3-litre, flat-6 engine, which generated 220bhp (a racing camshaft option could increase this to 240bhp).

ACCELERATION

0–60mph in 7 secs

MAXIMUM SPEED

160mph

PRODUCTION RUN

1,400

I did about five slow laps of Brooklands, by which time my arms were aching. I could only imagine the physical strength and endurance of the men who raced these cars in endurance events such as the Mille Miglia (1,000 miles, as its name suggests). The Carrera Panamericana was almost 2,000 miles! Add to that the heat of a continental race day and you have some idea of the physical stamina needed to race this car. The engine sounded better as my speed rose, and the car seemed to enjoy being driven hard. My lack of confidence on the track was entirely down to my limited ability as a driver, not to the car. One non-PC, contemporary review of the car, from *Car And Driver* in 1956, said, 'I cannot see it as anything but a man's machine. It's too hairy a beast for a woman to drive unless she's a fairly brawny athlete.' Another contemporary review said the 300 SL 'alarms the populace by its rapid acceleration.' Spoiled by the driver aids of the 21st century, I would therefore seem to qualify as 'not hairy enough' to drive the 300 SL far. Despite its age, the car still has a swift turn of pace.

The gearbox was surprisingly light, although you needed to be very accurate with shifts. But, hey, this car is 60 years old. The pouring rain didn't help and I actually felt guilty for taking the old girl out in such inclement weather. Ed, though, reassured me that 'she benefits from a run out now and again'.

I felt like I was driving a museum, though not in a bad way. It just felt like so much *history*. I managed to sneak five laps of the track before Ed needed to get the car back in the dry. As I climbed out, it felt like I was reluctantly leaving an old friend. The impact of experiencing the car in the flesh was huge. I parked her right next to her great-grandkid, an SLS AMG, and said goodbye. What a treat.

BELOW ***A high-spec SLS AMG next to the silver 300 SL, owned by Mercedes, which I took around the track.***

ABOVE ***The 1958 SL Roadsters were superlative successors to the 300 SL and elements of the latter also influenced the design of the W196 Grand Prix car and 300 SLR. The SLR was later to be involved in the worst motorsport disaster ever, at Le Mans in 1955, when 83 spectators as well as the driver were killed, with 120 others injured.***

The Gullwing not only changed car history in general, but it was also a very important turning point for Mercedes in particular. From being a brand known for solidly built, reliable saloons, the marque was suddenly perceived as a manufacturer of market-leading sports cars. Every SL Mercedes since the Gullwing bears some resemblance to the 300 SL, with their iconic grilles and elongated features.

And what of Max Hoffman's prediction that America would fall in love with the car? Well, he was right. Despite the fact that the Gullwing cost an eye-watering £4,796 (or $6,800) there was no shortage of takers. To put that price in context – in 1954, a family run-about cost roughly £450; a Jaguar XK140 was £1,598; and a Le Mans-winning Jaguar D Type was just £2,685. Of the 1,400 Gullwings made, more than 1,000 were sold in America. Automotive historians quote three different production totals: 1,485, 1,402 and 1,400. The correct total, including the light-alloy-bodied cars, was 1,400. The 300 SL was only available for two-and-a-half years.

In my opinion, there is no question that the 300 SL Gullwing is a game changer and a suitable starting point for any book about supercars. On 6 February 1954, when this car was first unveiled in New York's Regiment Armoury, the car world was changed instantly. The gullwing doors, direct fuel injection, independent suspension and the space-frame chassis were a major part of that, but there was also an overall sense of this stunning-looking car being historically significant. At that time, most average drivers were not especially aware of sports and GT cars. The 300 SL changed all that in a heartbeat. Nothing was ever the same again.

ABOVE **The 1950 Aston Martin DB2 Team Car.**

RIGHT **The Fiat 8V Zagato.**

Also in the 1950s

1950 Aston Martin DB2 The DB2 was a stunning car for the period, with a super-sleek profile.

1952 Fiat 8V Zagato A small two-seater, ideal for racing, the 8V Zagato used Italian coach-built bodywork.

1953 Corvette Entire books have been written about the Corvette and the car is indeed a cultural icon. Whether it qualifies as a supercar, though, is debatable. The first Corvette rolled off the production line in 1953 with the ambition of playing catch-up with Ford and Chrysler – what a brilliant response to their rivals! The reaction to the Corvette show model was so overwhelming that the production run was fast-tracked, going from clay model to actual car in just 15 months. The rest is history. Early incarnations were barely sports cars, never mind supercars, but the name and look of the 'Vette has endured for decades.

BELOW ***The legendary Corvette.***

The 1960s

LEFT ***The Lamborghini Miura – for many purists, the Year Zero for the modern supercar.***

In many ways, the 1960s were the years that defined the supercar. As the decade began, high-performance cars for the road were still largely versions, or adaptations, of race cars. Front engines were still universal, too. However, dramatic changes were afoot.

Britain's motor industry was enjoying huge demand for its modest family cars, but developments on the race track were starting to revolutionise the world of motorsport at the same time – with great consequences for the embryonic genre of supercars. Formula 1 had dabbled with moving the engine to a so-called 'mid-engine' layout – meaning it was located behind the driver but in front of the rear wheels. This offered better weight distribution and enabled the creation of sleeker cars with lowered centres of gravity. Then sports car racing teams started to experiment with the same idea – in Britain, geniuses such as Colin Chapman at Lotus and John Cooper were world-leaders in this dark art, and their revolutionary approach transformed the fortunes of British motorsport.

While the existing world-beaters – Ferrari, Ford et al – continued to make front-engined racers and road cars, there was one relatively new manufacturer hidden away, just up the road from Ferrari's Modena HQ, who had a different plan. This was a manufacturer that played no part in motor racing at all – deliberately so – yet it was about to steal the thunder from the big marques with a mid-engined layout that was very well favoured by race teams. The manufacturer was Lamborghini and the car in question was the 1966 Miura... a car that changed *everything*.

In the wake of the Miura, the supercar world would be forced to rip up all of its drawings and start again. Fortunately, at this time there was a burgeoning global economy, and so the world's wealthy were looking for something to spend their fortunes on. Consequently, the 1960s is a decade so full of important supercars – and great moments in supercar history – that we need to get stuck straight in.

1961 Jaguar E-Type

First things first: the Jaguar E-Type is widely regarded by many motoring experts as the most beautiful car of all time. Just look at it. Previous to this masterpiece, Italian cars tended to hold the mantle of 'best-looking', but the E-Type changed that *overnight*. Enzo Ferrari himself said it was, 'the most beautiful car ever made'.

The E-Type was launched in 1961 and caused an instant sensation. The car's designer, Malcolm Sayers, had previously worked on the D-Type race legend, and he made full use of that car's signature shape for the E-Type. To design the shape of the car, Sayers also used a wind tunnel for one of the first times in sports car history. (The wind tunnel used so much power that it could only be operated at night, to avoid causing local blackouts.) Sayers even went so far as to attach pieces of wool to certain points on the car, before test driver Norman Dewis raced off at 130mph. Sayers followed in a chase car to observe the effect of the wind on the tufts of wool, and so get an accurate impression of the car's aerodynamics. The E-type's looks, then, were informed by Sayer's obsessive attention to detail and meticulous knowledge of aerodynamics.

These incredible looks were complemented by first-class performance, with a top speed of 150mph (tested at the time on the M1 motorway). Although there were fast cars before the E-Type, as well as very stylish and well-engineered vehicles, too, fans of the E-Type argue that this was the first time all of these elements had been put together in one package.

What's more, the car continued a Jaguar tradition of innovation, with a central steel monocoque, which was far lighter than that of its rivals – again, heavily influenced by the Le Mans-winning D-Type. The car had independent rear suspension, which created a far more luxurious ride than harsher contemporary sports car set-ups, disc brakes (though they were not always that sharp), and an array of other mechanical innovations. As a result, handling, cornering, and steering were all immaculate.

The E-Type commands a fierce loyalty from its fans, and during the course of writing this book I was pressured – widely – to include it in my ten game changers. For sure, it could be argued that the E-Type's revolutionary aerodynamics, alone, qualify it as a game changer, and for that reason – if no other – it could be included in my top ten. It is telling that designer Malcolm Sayer did not like to be titled as such, instead preferring to be called an aerodynamicist. The Museum of Modern Art in New York would agree, as it holds one of the cars in its permanent collection.

In the early 1960s, there were numerous cars that could top the 150mph mark, but when the E-Type was launched, it was the fastest car in the world. Incredibly, at a price of £2,097 ($3,536), the E-Type cost just

one-third of the price of the equivalent Ferrari (the preceding XK120 had also been very competitively priced).

If a supercar is a vehicle that attracts its own celebrity – and, by extension, celebrity owners – then the E-Type is without parallel. During the 1960s, the car was an essential ornament for a string of high-profile names such as Steve McQueen, George Best, Brigitte Bardot and Tony Curtis. This was the car that in many ways defined the Swinging Sixties. And it seems the E-Type's appeal continues to last, with the car consistently winning various 'Best Looking Car Ever' polls. The E-Type has become a favourite of classic car collector's, with prices exploding upwards, year after year.

ABOVE ***The E-Type wasn't just beautiful; it had serious performance statistics, too. As a result, the car enjoyed a successful racing life (pictured). Later, a lightweight version of the E-Type was tuned for racing. It had aluminium panels and an increased horsepower of 300bhp. Only 12 of these were ever made (so, if your grandad hasone in his garage, tell him he needs to review his insurance policy).***

The E-Type may be regarded by many as a sports car, not a supercar, but having researched this piece, and fully realised just what an amazing car it is, I would press anyone to revise that opinion.

SUPERCAR FACT
The Prancing Horse – known as the Cavallino Rampante, originated from an Italian flying ace who used it on his aircraft. The emblem also features the colours of the Italian flag, while yellow is the colour of Modena town – home to the Ferrari factory.

1962 Ferrari 250GTO

The 250GTO is considered by many to be the ultimate Ferrari to own. Originally made in 1962, less than 40 cars were ever built. The GTO was made to race and its stripped out, no-frills style – added to its surprising ease of use – makes it of great appeal to purists. The car was actually an evolution of the 250GT SWB – refined to have better aerodynamic properties and more power – and was initially built to take part in the FIA's new GT championship, so the basic but lightweight set-up features a highly tuned 3-litre V12 engine and aluminium panels riveted to a tubular chassis. The formula worked – the 250GTO won the GT series three years in a row and frequently defeated all-comers in its class at Le Mans.

It was designed by Bizzarrini, with bodywork by Scaglietti. Despite its latterday record-breaking values, the front-engined 250GTO was not really a game changer in supercar terms. However, it has retrospectively become *the* Ferrari to own, with world record prices edging past £30 million ($50 million) in some cases. The car is now considered to be so important to

BELOW ***Nick Mason's beautiful GTO. Note the number plate.***

ABOVE ***The 250GTO was based on the Testarossa sports racing cars that saw so much racing success during the late 1950s. 'GTO' stands for 'Gran Turismo Omologato'.***

Ferrari's heritage that photos of the 250GTO are still occasionally used to help sell new models.

Pink Floyd drummer and renowned car collector Nick Mason kindly showed me his famous GTO, seen here. I asked him why he was drawn to buy such an icon. 'I'm not actually the world's greatest supercar fan. I prefer the older cars, and for me the GTO is fascinating. It has become a supercar in a way, because of the value, but I wouldn't really call it a supercar, because they can have a tinge of total impracticality about them. The GTO, on the other hand, is a tool for winning a race series. It is because it looks so great that it's become a supercar.

'I first saw them racing at Goodwood in 1964 and I thought they looked unbelievable. I actually took photos of the car that I now own. From then on, I could draw the lines of a GTO from memory. They were race winners but people were more interested in racing Formula 1 cars, things like that. The GTOs are quite a specialist part of the racing scene.

'Once I had some money I bought a 275GTB/4, which was hard work. Eventually, I was able to buy this GTO [pictured left]. I had put the word out and, when I found it, it was a lot of money – fully restored, in perfect condition. I had never driven one before. I tend to buy cars entirely on an emotional impulse. With most of my best cars, it never occurs to me to drive them before buying. I once bought a Bugatti chassis I had found leaning against a chicken shed. The GTO was emotional in the same way. Obviously, when great drivers are telling you a car is magnificent, you take their word for it. So I did and I bought it.

'There are elements that appeal to the schoolboy. The spoiler doesn't really work much, for instance, but it's so purposeful – it's the beginning of the idea of the rear wing. The Testarossa and the P4 are also contenders for the greatest Ferrari ever, but the GTO is right up there. The thing that gives this car the edge is the usability. I like people driving it, because if you like cars you 'get' the GTO. If you wind it up a bit, it is the most perfect amateur's racing car, a really nice balance of brakes, chassis, power – you can get the tail out and not lose it. You can show off in it a bit. I drive it in London – possible because the clutch is really light. One winter in town there was a lot of snow and I couldn't get my other practical cars to start, so I took the kids to school in the GTO.' To be fair to Nick, that's some way to turn up at the school gates!

1962 AC Shelby Cobra 427

Carroll Shelby was a former chicken farmer and a successful racing driver who had won Le Mans in 1959, and who would go on to work with Ford on numerous high-performance projects. Born with a heart condition, Shelby had to take a daily dose of nitroglycerine pills throughout his life. After his race career ended, he began importing the AC Ace – a little British sports car with 1950s styling – into the American market. Shelby felt, however, that the little Ace was under-powered and he was convinced that he could wring more out of its set-up. So, he called Ace up and asked if they could fit – or rather cram – a massive Ford 427 V8 engine into the little car (427 cubic inches, hence the name). Somehow, they managed it. Due to the small size of the car relative to the huge 425bhp engine, the power-to-weight ratio was ludicrous, and the subsequent acceleration was breathtaking. As a result, the car would hold the world record for the quickest 0–60mph sprint, 4.2 seconds, for two decades. It took just ten seconds to go zero to 100mph.

This trans-Atlantic collaboration wasn't just a drag racer, though. The new car's muscular curves allowed for great aerodynamics, and it handled

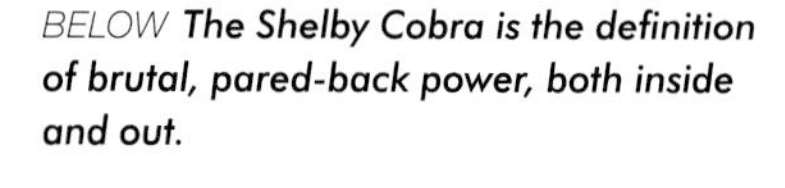

BELOW ***The Shelby Cobra is the definition of brutal, pared-back power, both inside and out.***

ABOVE ***Classic muscular looks and massive amounts of raw power make the Shelby Cobra a brutish classic.***

brilliantly. The Cobra raced very successfully, winning every event it entered in US motorsport. In Europe it was less successful, usually struggling against the might of the Ferrari 250GTO. Shelby was not a man to lose easily, however, so in 1964 he created the AC Daytona Coupe – essentially a heavily modified Cobra with better aerodynamics and even more power – with the specific aim of beating the 250GTO. He took it to Le Mans and won the GT class at the first attempt.

The original AC Cobra was a ridiculously successful car, made all the more remarkable because it came from such a very small manufacturer. A limited number were sold as race cars, which command huge prices today. The Cobra is also one of the most copied and replicated supercars of all-time. Many fans consider it to be a landmark supercar because of the decision to squeeze *so much* power into such a small car. That capacity, plus its muscular looks and enigmatic presence, really do make this a one-off in the supercar world.

GAME CHANGER

1963 Porsche 911

I AM STANDING IN A FIELD IN A GREY, wind-swept corner of Northampton, in the English Midlands. It is a flat, mostly rural county, and at times the rain feels horizontal. On one side of me is a rock star who sells out stadiums; on the other is a man who made his fortune making shoes. I am in the middle, familiar with neither footwear fortunes nor singing to stadiums, just books and words. And fast cars. Along with the hundreds of other petrol-heads gathered here at Silverstone, we all have one thing in common: the Porsche 911.

We are at this iconic British racetrack for the car's 50th anniversary celebrations. The original plan had been to gather 911 examples of what

ABOVE ***The supercar world's most enduring silhouette: the Porsche 911.***

ABOVE **The Porsche 911-991, the latest generation of the icon. The 911 is the supercar exception that proves the rule, defying almost all engineering Golden Rules and certainly flying in the face of both its age and fashion.**

many consider the most unique of all supercars. In actual fact, more than 1,050 cars have turned up. The cheapest examples are a little battered, even tired-looking, and would set you back only a few thousand quid. On this day, however, they share the same mud as examples worth well over £1 million ($1.7 million).

On a superficial level, we know we are all here for a birthday party – but drilling deeper I realise there is more to it than that. Going by most definitions of a modern supercar, the Porsche 911 does not qualify for this book. Why? Well, at least superficially, it is a car stuck in a time warp. It stubbornly refuses to change. It is still, after more than 50 years, rear-engined. It has a flat-6, 'boxer' engine (so called because the cylinders lie horizontal and punch back and forth like a boxer's jab). As the 911 heads into its sixth decade, it still has a shape that is immediately recognisable when parked alongside its 1963 predecessor. So, how and why has the 911 lasted five decades in a supercar genre in which five years is considered an age? Bugatti critics, for instance, decry the fact that the Veyron was launched in 2005, and at the time of writing it has yet to be replaced. In 'Porsche 911 years', that's the time-frame for a minor facelift. And yet, for all this, the 911 was one of the very first cars that made it onto the list when I was compiling my supercar garage on paper.

How can this be?

First, a mini-history lesson: back in the 1930s and 1940s, a young German by the name of Ferdinand Porsche was into making his own toys. It was perhaps no surprise that he showed signs of an engineering bent, considering his grandad was not exactly the type to go fly-fishing and crown green bowling. Instead, Gramps founded the car design company, Porsche, in 1931. Shortly afterwards, he began designing a racing car for which he had no customer and virtually no money to spend on development. Then he was asked by Adolf Hitler, car fan and all-round genocidal megalomaniac, to design a 'People's Car', or 'Volkswagen'. Porsche Senior did exactly that and his new little car – the VW Beetle – became an enduring masterpiece. Just after the end of the Second World War, the first car bearing his surname was launched: the Porsche 356. Porsche planned to make 1,500 of them. He eventually sold 78,000. A glorious racing career also followed for his new marque, with Porsche cars establishing themselves as ingeniously designed and prodigiously quick.

LEFT ***26 July 2013, at Silverstone race track, Northampton, England. Over 1,000 examples of the 911 take part in a record-breaking parade of the famous car. The front row features the new Turbo and GT3 models.***

So, we have established that Ferdinand Porsche had a pretty cool grandad. Unfortunately, Gramps died when young Ferdinand – known by his nickname of Butzi – was only 16. Butzi's own dad was also an engineer within the blossoming family car firm and it was almost pre-destined that the young lad would follow in those footsteps, despite his early academic prospects not being good. Butzi was kicked out of one engineering school because the tutors felt he was simply not gifted in engineering. The family car company, though, disagreed – and so he started work at Porsche in 1956.

And what was the first major car project that he designed?

The 911.

He was only in his mid-twenties at the time.

ABOVE **The Porsche 911 connoisseur's dream car – the fabled 2.7 RS.**

ABOVE ***A very early example, circa 1964, with a modest engine and minimal driver aids. Despite this, the 911's shape and finesse soon attracted a very broad appeal. It wasn't just for gentleman racers.***

At the 911's launch in 1963, at the Frankfurt Motor Show, some observers were puzzled by this curious little car. It had four seats (a so-called 2+2, as the rear ones were rather petite), an engine in the rear – in a genre where the majority of sports car production still used front-engined layouts – and yet its curvaceous, sloping lines were immediately distinct for the time. However, Peugeot's lawyers were not impressed with the new car's name. It was initially called a Porsche 901, but the French legal eagles very kindly 'pointed out' that Peugeot had worldwide rights to any car name with a zero in the middle. So, Porsche simply substituted a '1' and the 911 was born.

Fifty years later, over 820,000 examples of the 911 have been sold, making it the most commercially successful Top Ten supercar in this book. This sounds like a lot of cars, but actually it is a relatively limited production run. The entire VW car group makes that many vehicles in three weeks. This limitation in number only adds to the car's relative exclusivity. No other supercar bears such a resemblance to a launch model made half a century previously. However, what appears on the surface to be a complete anomaly, within the realm of car design, is actually simply a case of a car that proved to be so unique, so well conceived, and so enjoyable to drive and own that it simply didn't need to be continually and profoundly re-invented. The 911's rear-mounted, flat-6 engine set-up has provided driving thrills adored by its owners for generation after generation. Some things have changed, however. Starting off at just 130bhp back in 1963, half a century later the 991 Turbo S of 2014 boasts a jaw-dropping 560bhp. (Some 911 GT2 models are now so fast that they have been christened 'Widowmakers'.) Although these power plants are a world apart in terms of pure performance, the engines are essentially still close relatives.

Maybe the reason for the 911's longevity is that famous Ferry Porsche-designed shape. It was certainly radical in the early 1960s and yet, somehow, despite all the years since, that timeless historical design still looks as ultra-modern as any other sports car on the market. And there's also a certain understated, and very appealing, aura of confidence about a car which refuses to fundamentally alter its form for so long. In car design, half a century is an age. Yet the 911 has seen just three new platforms across seven versions in 50 years. Only a very few select contemporaries in car design, music, culture, fashion – in fact any field – from that period are still so highly esteemed today, and yet also based on such original and long-standing principles of design.

The 911 is a car of contradictions, too, yet these contrasts serve only to further fuel its popularity. It is practical yet sporty, beautiful yet functional, traditional yet innovative. Elsewhere, the 911's driving position is beloved by many – the way it cocoons the body so perfectly. Also heralded is the practicality of what is such a powerful sports car – 'the everyday supercar', to quote a cliché. Equally championed are the various derivatives such as the whale-fins, Targas, and so on. Each different version rolls off the tongue of purists like rare vinyl records or precious artefacts. Some adore the early models, while many say the 1980s was a high watermark. Others love the

BELOW ***The RSR is one of the rarest examples of the breed, with race-winning examples later being sold on to road-going customers. Less than 30 cars were sold in total. Current resale values can be in excess of £1 million ($1.68 million).***

pure sports car heritage. Some just love the fact that in an industry where designers, marketing experts and accountants now tinker with every aspect of a new car, the 911 has been left relatively untouched and pure. *Das ist nicht kaputt...*

There is, however, a downside to this odd, almost trainspotter-ish appeal. 911s also attract so-called 'purists' like antique collectors at a stately home boot sale. This fanaticism meant that when the air-cooled 911 (internally known as a 993) was replaced with a water-cooled, new model (the 996), the outrage could be measured on the Richter scale. The fact that the manufacturer had used the same, tear-drop headlights – on this latest 911 model – as the ones they put on the (far cheaper) Boxster two-seater was an insult too horrific for the ardent 911 fans to bear. Well, for some, anyway. Leap forward to the new 911 (991) and nothing has changed. The new 911 GT3 will not be available with a manual gearbox, simply because the sublime Porsche PDK double clutch gearbox is so exceptionally good. There is no point having a new version of the car with a clunky stick shift. Cue further shrieks of horror from purists and more ruffled feathers than could ever be created by a fox in a battery chicken farm. And I am sure you'll want to know all about the pros and cons of the hydraulic steering system being replaced with a controversial electro-magnetic one? No? Oh, well, you can guess what happened when *that* feature was revealed.

However, and this is the nub of the car's legend, when you sit inside a 911, all of that chatter, that history, that provenance, all those arguments and those gentle evolutions are simultaneously ultra-sensitised and forgotten. Once you put your foot down in a Porsche 911, the addictive nature of the driving experience overrides everything else. When you fire up a 911 you

ABOVE ***Porsche's rich racing heritage underpins the 911's enduring appeal. From touring car championships to the all-conquering 917 Le Mans legend of the 1970s, Porsche can draw upon its glittering past to inject its future models with an exemplary pedigree.***

RIGHT ***Many purists see the GT3 derivation of the 911 as the perfect choice, being a two-seater road-going racer, brutally stripped-out to be as lightweight and rapid as possible, complete with aerodynamic body kit and extensive engine tuning. However, the GT3's more frightening older brother, the GT2 (seen here), is the so-called 'Widowmaker'.***

are also engaging in a deeply personal event. You are inheriting all those decades of motorsport and automotive heritage, and in the process creating your own little slice of car history. As I wrote in the Introduction to this book, this is because each fan has a *relationship* with their 911.

The 911 has a unique chemistry in an industry where super-computers and mass-production constantly strive to achieve clinical perfection in engineering. Its chemistry defies description. The 911 creates a feeling that is emotional, visceral, even *physical* at times.

So *that* is why we are all standing in a windy field in Northampton, as I finish off a greasy hot dog and clutch a can of Diet Coke with cold fingers. Just after lunch, the call goes out to get in our vehicles. We slowly file on to the famous Silverstone tarmac in strict order, ready for a man with a flag to wave us off on a glorious parade lap. Over 1,000 examples of a car that is 50 years old then glide around a racing circuit made famous the world over, while two Spitfires perform aerial tricks and a stunning fly-by. Directly in front of me is a 911 worth £600,000 ($1 million); behind me is one worth a more modest £5,000 ($8,400).

For its longevity, its unique layout in the supercar world, but mostly for its sheer presence, the 911 is a game changer.

The 911 is an anomaly. It flies in the face of almost every supercar 'rule'.

Only it's not 'just' a supercar, is it?

It's a 911.

Porsche 911

LAUNCHED

1963

POWER

130bhp back in 1963 (half a century later, the 991 Turbo S of 2014 boasts a jaw-dropping 560bhp

ACCELERATION

0–60mph in 8.3 secs

MAXIMUM SPEED

130mph

PRODUCTION RUN

820,00 sold to date

GAME CHANGER

1966 Lamborghini Miura

ABOVE **_The Lamborghini Miura made every contemporary supercar that preceded it suddenly look old-fashioned._**

ON ONE OF LONDON'S MOST prestigious streets there is an astonishing building housing the headquarters of the Royal Automobile Club. Established in 1897, the Club's history mirrors that of the motorcar itself, having been involved in the very early days of motorsport – and even introducing the first driving licence. The building, in Pall Mall, is an Aladdin's cave of glorious antiques, period furniture, sublime interior design and architecture, all framed by oil paintings of famous cars and racing drivers, as well as the occasional portrait of a member of the Royal family. It reeks of history and fine craftsmanship, of artisan skills honed over decades and decades – of an historical *eye for detail.*

I had been invited here to see a car that was in situ inside this grand headquarters. As I walked excitedly through the revolving door from the busy London street, I was confronted by a flowing staircase, which leads to a carpeted rotunda at the heart of the building. And there, roped off and surrounded by cabinets brimming with antiques and motor sport trophies, was one of the most striking pieces of craftsmanship that even this great institution has ever seen: a flame orange, absolutely pristine Lamborghini Miura.

Standing to the side of the car was the owner, the delightfully genial and welcoming Peter Read, a former accountant who now possesses one of the world's finest supercar collections. We chatted about the interminable rain, but quickly the talk turned to the Lamborghini in front of us. How had Peter come across this car?

'I had previously owned a Miura S, a right-hand drive model. I'd had all sorts of problems with the carburettors and eventually I just gave up and put a fuel injection on it, but of course it then ceased to be original. I was then made an offer I couldn't refuse by a famous car collector, whose wife liked the colour, and so I sold it. Almost immediately I thought, *What have I done?!* So I set about tracking down a spectacular example to right the wrong. This Miura is that car.'

This elusive appeal, this legendary, almost seductive persona that the Miura has is inextricably linked with Lamborghini as a brand – but also with its namesake and founder, Ferruccio Lamborghini. The Miura is as rich in history and provenance as perhaps any other supercar.

The Lamborghini story starts, incredibly, not with high-performance cars but with tractors, air-conditioning units and gas heaters. This is how Ferruccio Lamborghini made his money in post-war northern Italy, initially using mechanical spares and army surplus supplies. He had served as a mechanic in the Italian RAF during the war, and on leaving had quickly displayed a very creative engineering brain and business acumen. The son of viticulturalists (wine makers), the young Ferruccio used to tend his own

LEFT Gandini, designer of the Miura, also had a hand in the design of iconic cars such as the Maserati Khamsin (pictured), the Ferrari 308GT/4, the Lancia Stratos and the Alfa Romeo Carabo.

SUPERCAR FACT

The Alfa Romeo Carabo – also designed by Gandini – is a shocking and striking early supercar silhouette. First seen at the Paris Auto Show in late 1968, it is one of the very first cars to use upswinging 'scissor' doors.

vineyard on a tractor his firm had built. Once the tractor, air-conditioning and gas heater business had started to make serious money, Ferruccio – like many red-blooded continentals of the period – started buying expensive cars. Ferraris were of particular interest, such as the 250GT that he owned. He even competed in the Mille Miglia in 1948.

However, Ferruccio felt the Ferraris were not refined enough and that they were essentially just race cars for the road. So, he started to believe there was a need for a more luxurious and sophisticated GT car, or 'grand tourer'. Lamborghini legend then tells the tale of how a clutch on one of his Ferraris broke. Being an engineer, Ferruccio noticed that it was essentially the same construction as the clutch on one of his tractors. Ferruccio asked Enzo Ferrari directly for a replacement and – so the story goes – Ferrari said Ferruccio knew nothing about supercars and should stick to building tractors. Mr Lamborghini did stick to building tractors, but he also took that as a personal snub and started building supercars, too. He founded Lamborghini Automobili in 1961 when he was just 45, basing himself in Sant'Agata Bolognese, less than 20 miles from the Ferrari factory.

Ferruccio's initial ambition was to build a refined GT car that would not be designed for racing, but specifically for road use. As such, he flew in the face of high-performance car manufacturer convention and chose not to race his creations. Lamborghini did not race any of their cars until the

ABOVE ***Following on from this debut version, Lamborghini later made a Miura S with a stiffer chassis and more power, followed by an even more powerful 'SV', and a one-off roadster that never made it into full production.***

1980s. Ferruccio's first car was the stylish 350GT, of 1964, built in just four months and unveiled in October 1963 at the Turin Motor Show. Due to a legal problem the engine was not in the car so, allegedly, Ferruccio filled the engine bay with bricks so that the car would sit low enough. He then spent much of the show making sure no one looked under the bonnet! The 350GT was well received and met with a very positive response from an intrigued car world. The rumour was that he sold each car at a loss just to compete with Ferrari and get his name known. Eventually, he would sell 120 350GTs. The debut car was followed by the lesser-known 400GT (essentially an evolution of the 350) and then a 400GT 2+2. Both were well received, but back at the Lamborghini factory something far more significant was just beginning.

The Lamborghini design team of Dallara, Stanzani and Wallace had been working on a revolutionary idea in their own time, squirrelled away from Ferruccio's gaze, initially because they feared it might not be a concept he would naturally agree to. There has been some debate over exactly who worked on the Miura. The important thing is this: whichever creative brains did it made the monumental decision to take an engine layout that was highly popular in motor racing at the time – the mid-engined configuration – and use it in their new road car. This was something that had never before been tried in a high-performance road car. Porsche had recently launched their rear-engined 911 and Ferrari were heavily in favour of front-engine cars. However – as mentioned earlier – in the world of racing, the genius of people such as Colin Chapman at Lotus, in England, had started to realise

BELOW ***Seen with both flung open, the Miura's distinctive doors represent the horns of a bull.***

the benefits of a mid-engined layout. Numerous F1 cars used the idea, as did rival marques in creating race cars such as the Ferrari 250LM. There was also a Bugatti Type 235 racing in Grand Prix, for a short time, that was transversely mounted. However, this approach had not yet been used on a high performance, road-going car. Enter the Miura.

Ferruccio initially believed that no Lamborghini should ever be rear- or mid-engined. However, when the team working on the new design showed him their ideas, he felt it might be a useful marketing exercise. He therefore gave the project the green light, christening it the P400 (for 'posteriore', meaning 'behind', and 4.0 litre). In so doing, he effectively rubber-stamped the world's first mid-engined supercar.

Excited by the possibilities, Lamborghini showed a rolling chassis only (that is with no bodywork) at the Turin Motor Show in 1965. The press and customer reaction was striking. Despite only being a bare chassis, with no bodywork, several customers actually placed orders on the spot! Buoyed by the reaction, Ferruccio signed off a full production plan and handed the task of creating a striking bodywork shell to the Bertone design company. They, in turn, handed the project to a 25-year-old designer called Marcello Gandini.

BELOW LEFT *The famous Miura 'eyelashes'.*

BELOW RIGHT *The famous design house Bertone has had their hand in some of the world's most iconic supercars, and the Miura was no exception.*

In central London, Lamborghini have a dealership in upmarket South Kensington, and in the glass-fronted showroom is a man named Steve Higgins. Immaculately dressed, larger-than-life, and intimately knowledgeable about all Lamborghinis – as well as all supercars – Steve is rightly revered in the supercar world. He takes up the story: 'Gandini

ABOVE ***Lamborghini had no test track so all their cars were regularly seen flying at high speeds along the roads near the Sant'Agato factory.***

designed just the most beautiful thing. Because of the way that Lamborghini was – it wasn't the richest car company in the world, they hadn't really built a proper supercar before, just those GTs – they had some financial constraints to work to. For example, Lamborghini did not have a test track of its own, but that was never considered a problem because the cars were intended for the road, not a track. So, you would see these amazing concepts thrashing around the roads near the factory!

'In a sense, Gandini was relatively inexperienced, but creatively that meant he didn't know what he *couldn't* do. Once he had created that amazing silhouette, the technical restraints of his design had to be overcome. However, that is part of the charm. Being a young designer with little experience – and, most importantly, not being told what to do – meant he could just let his imagination go crazy. The result is this amazing design. In many people's eyes, the Miura is the most beautiful car of all-time. It's absolutely delicious.'

Named after the renowned Spanish bullfighter, Antonio Miura, the car took the bull theme to extremes (Ferruccio himself was a Taurus, incidentally). The Miura's logo was a bull's tail, and the ends of the doors curve skywards in a little flick of metal – which seems rather odd unless you look at the car from the front and see that it is mimicking a bull's horns. Gandini said the Miura was a synthesis of 1950s and 1960s sports cars, 'interpreted in a modern way'.

The Miura stunned the motoring world when it was launched at the 1966 Geneva Motor Show. It was an instant, huge hit – an overnight sensation. However, had show-goers looked under the (locked) bonnet, they would have found another load of ballast hiding there in place of the engine, which had once again not been ready in time. This mattered not one jot. Even priced at an eye-watering £8,050, or $13,575 (at a time when an E-Type cost less than £2,000, or $3,400, remember), the order book quickly filled up. The Miura was the fastest production car in the world on its launch. For many, it is the very first supercar, if you discount front-engined vehicles. The car proceeded to redefine supercar history and is now widely recognised as the very first mid-engined supercar.

So, as I walked through those doors off Pall Mall and up the stairs to shake Peter Read's hand, and talk to him about his Miura, all this incredible history was swimming around in my head.

Peter had had the car restored in Italy by some of the original artisans who had worked with Lamborghini in the 1960s. So, I knew how he had come across the car and why it looked so perfect. But *why* did he want to buy a Miura?

BELOW ***A transversely mounted engine is one that is rotated through 90 degrees, rather than running in line with the car. This was how Lamborghini managed to fit the big V12 Miura engine into a smaller road car. Also, the engine block, crankcase and transmission were all in one extremely complicated alloy casting – similar in fact to the front-engined, transversely mounted Mini.***

'I became interested in sports cars when I was a youngster and bought my first one – a Lotus Elan – when I was at university. During the summer, I worked on a building site and earned £700. I then saw a Lotus Elan for sale for £690 ($1,160), so I bought it! I've still got it. Different cars interest me. I have had a good career so I was able to buy them. The Elan gave way to a Europa, but I kept the Elan and that set me on the slippery slope of owning multiple cars. I had a few 911s, including a Turbo, but always hankered after a Ferrari, so I started with a 328, then a Testarossa, then a 355 GTS and a Daytona, too. Then I went mad and bought an F40. But the Miura... well, the Miura is a historical landmark. So, if you collect supercars, you are inevitably drawn towards owning one.'

Standing next to the car makes all photos of the Miura feel rather pointless. The feminine lines of the car are reinforced by the 'eyelashes' around the pop-up headlights. The absolute precision of the design is exemplified by the crisp shut lines, although on some early cars these were so tight that when opening the bonnet the panels were likely to clash. The front fenders are more muscular than you might expect and rise up either side of a ribline running down the centre of the bonnet. The rear has a subtle ducktail – one of the first examples of this supercar feature – and below that is some venting with a hexagonal theme in black (a design that would inspire the Aventador some 45 years later). The sills tend to be silver or gold, while the large air-intake scoops – by the rear wheels – add a sense of power.

Peter offered to let me climb in, and after I had hastily pushed him out of the way I pressed the door switch and nestled down into the low seats.

The Miura is just 41.5 inches high, which in the context of muscle cars and bigger GT sports cars was a sensation (the Ford GT40 was, as its name suggests, an exception at an even lower 40 inches). The mid-engined layout means the driver's seat is situated unusually far forward, which also altered the rear overhang of the car, both aspects of which were revolutionary. The overhang also allowed for a half-decent boot, unheard of in most supercars. Underneath this boot the exhaust tips are not actually connected to the main pipes. If they were connected, the exhaust would snap off whenever you lifted the rear end to inspect the engine.

Sitting in a Miura is a snug place to be. The most notable feature is the wrap-around windscreen, which seems futuristic now, never mind in 1966. The car has a metal-gated gear lever with a rear finger groove for comfort, and numerous analogue dials. Near the rear-view mirror are a series of jumbo jet-like flick switches which operate, among other things, the lights and fans.

Behind your head is that famous V12 engine, and in Peter's car there is a clear panel to show you the carburettors. Or, as Peter explains, 'So you can see when it catches fire!'

But what is this legend of the supercar world actually like to drive?

'On a dual carriageway it's quite easy,' explains Peter. 'However, manoeuvring it much is a real pig. To be fair, that's largely down to my shape, because my legs are too long! My knees end up in the air and if I move forward to see out of the side I smack my head on the windscreen. But I don't think early supercars were necessarily designed to be easy to drive, were they?

'Visibility out of the back is okay, straight out of the front is alright, too, but the thing you notice is that it hasn't got any wing mirrors. The early ones didn't bother with that. In traffic that is a nightmare, and in particular coming on to the slip road of a motorway can be dicey. Mind you, in 1966 everyone else was driving Morris Minors so it didn't matter – because no one ever overtook you!'

One aspect of the Miura that this book cannot do justice to is the sound of the V12. It is incredible. There is a neat contrast between the very muscular note of the engine and the very sensual, curvaceous bodywork. All of these things make the Miura a very special supercar. For many, it is the greatest ever. It certainly makes my Top Ten with ease. At the time of its creation, the Miura was widely recognised to have eclipsed Ferrari, and perhaps it even made those cars look out of date. The front-engined Ferrari 365 GTB/4 Daytona would stick with a front engine and looked almost conservative by comparison. It is a fact that Lamborghini beat Ferrari to the mid-engined V12 market. It is also a fact that several manufacturers had been vying to be the first to be mid-engined, but that Lamborghini got there first. The Miura certainly made Lamborghini a serious player in the supercar field. Many aspects of the car set the benchmark for future supercars: the mid-engine, the ducktail, the curves, the quad-cam, the looks...

Yes, the cabin noise was quite high, because of the engine layout. Yes, there were stories of the rather terrifying, high-speed front-end lift of that pointed, low-snooping nose (particularly as the front-sited fuel tank emptied

BELOW ***The Miura: the original modern supercar?***

of petrol). Yes, the sheet steel chassis, which showcased Italian metalworker skills so well, was said to flex under high-speed strain. And on 1960s roads, often in states of disrepair, the suspension was not exactly cushioning. Yes, this was not a perfect car by any means.

But, frankly, who cares?

When you walk past the entrance to the RAC building, you have no idea of the wealth of motoring history that lies behind its doors. Those antique cabinets, brimming with trophies, represent all the decades of races, cars, engineers, drivers, and automotive brilliance. In the same way, the Miura represents decades of supercars, perhaps like no other. The engine layout, the bodywork, the finish, the spirit of the Miura – all are so definitive, so game-changing and symbolic of the supercar genre. This has almost become a beacon for everything that is thrilling about the notion of a car that goes fast and – at the same time – looks absolutely, jaw-droppingly beautiful.

Lamborghini Miura

LAUNCHED
1966

POWER
350bhp

ACCELERATION
0–60mph in 7 secs

MAXIMUM SPEED
171mph

PRODUCTION RUN
It is thought that approximately 750 Miuras were produced, though this is unverified.

73

Also in the 1960s

1966 Ford GT40 For much of the 1950s and start of the 1960s, Ferrari dominated motor racing. By contrast, Ford was an automotive powerhouse commercially, but it could just not compete with the Italian marque on the track. So, following the old adage of 'if you can't beat 'em, join 'em', Ford decided to buy Ferrari. Protracted negotiations began in 1964 and a deal was set up. However, at the last minute Enzo Ferrari pulled out of the deal. Henry Ford was furious and vowed to take revenge on the track. Ford injected so many resources into the resulting car that noted author Eric Dymock later called the GT40 'the automotive equivalent of NASA's moon project'.

The result was the incredible Ford GT40, so-called, as already mentioned, because it was just 40.5 inches high (measure that on a wall and stand next to it!). The GT40 initially adopted an embryonic design by the English racing company Lola, who had been brought on board to help fast-track the project. In order for the new racing car to meet eligibility criteria for Le Mans, Ford had to build 50 road-going versions. So, they created a 4.7-litre V-8 capable of 335bhp, with a top speed of 164mph. After a few early scares – one GT40 went airborne at 150mph on a bend – the car's race potential shone through. On the track, however, the performance was considerably greater (speeds of up to 207mph) and Ford must have thoroughly enjoyed their ultimate revenge against the Ferraris when the

LEFT ***The Ford GT40's doors were cut into the roof.***

LEFT ***The Ford GT40 MKII at the Road America Elkheart Lake race track. This car, driven by Bruce McLaren and Chris Amon, won the 1966 Le Mans 24 Hour race.***

GT40 won Le Mans four years in a row – from 1966 to 1969. In the first of those triumphs, the car even scooped the top three places, cementing its reputation as a genuine racing superstar.

For all its track success, some reviewers cheekily said it was the car whose owner you wouldn't want your daughter to marry. Less humourous critics decried the poor interior build quality, with an appalled *CAR* magazine writer sneering at the rough-cut carpets, 'phoney' leather trim and fascia paint that looked like it had been applied with 'a loo brush'. Other critics said it had 'sloppy road manners', which clearly went against Ford's claim that this was 'the ultimate road car'. Somehow, though, the stunning exterior made you forget about all of this.

In 2004, a revised version of the GT40 was launched, with the intention of sharpening Ford's rather staid global image. This modern-day version would be called, simply, the 'GT' (partly because it was three inches higher, partly over naming rights issues). Many people consider the original, 1960s road-going version of the GT40 to be the 'first' supercar. However, because it was essentially a road-going dilution of a racing car, others are less convinced. In either case, alongside the Model T, the GT40 has staked its claim as one of the most famous Fords of all.

1960 Aston Martin DB4 GT Zagato This car was made by a company that initially worked out of a shed in Newport Pagnell, in England. Incredibly Aston Martin evolved into one of the world's greatest-ever brands, creating cars such as this stunningly refined British masterpiece.

BELOW ***The 1962 Aston Martin DB4 Superleggera.***

ABOVE **The 1963 Ferrari Superamerica.**

1961 Ferrari 400GT Superamerica Each Superamerica was built-to-order for the customer, with individual detailing. It was, and remains, a brutally fast car.

1963 Aston Martin DB5 An awesome, front-engined British car, made extremely famous by a fictional driver called James Bond. It is, fittingly, very civilised and refined, with electric windows and optional air conditioning. The bulletproof panels, oil slick gadget, machine guns, rotating licence plates, ejector seat, radar, and telescopic tyre slashers were one-off optional extras ordered personally by a man called Q. (The car's successor, the DB6, was more like a Jaws to the DB5's Bond.)

1963 Ferrari 250LM The 250 series of Ferraris had many variants – the 1963 'LM' put the engine behind the driver to achieve its mid-engined, 3.3-litre V12 layout. It is significant as the very first road-going, mid-engined Ferrari V12. The long tail overhang, necessary to accommodate the mid-engined layout, might look odd in photos – but in the flesh it is stunning. Up until the more luxurious versions of the 250 series, the experience of driving most Ferraris was simply like being in a race car.

1965 Ferrari 275GTB The 275GTB was a perfectly proportioned, front-engined, classic GT car. It didn't sell all that well, though (see the Daytona).

1965 Iso Grifo A3C Designed by Bizzarrini, this was a race version of the AC3 that won its Le Mans class in 1965.

1966 Jensen FF The Jensen FF was Britain's supercar pretender to the crown and was the first production GT sports car with four-wheel drive. FF stood for 'Ferguson Formula', the name of the 4WD system. The FF also launched Dunlop's anti-lock braking system, leading some critics to call this 'the world's safest car'. The Interceptor was a similarly sporty Jensen.

1967 Shelby Mustang GT500 (Eleanor from the film *Gone In 60 Seconds*) A tuned-up Mustang created by Shelby, the GT500 had 'only' 355bhp, but was designed to be a more everyday car than its stripped-back GT350 sibling.

1967 Maserati Ghibli One of Maserati's finest cars, the Ghibli had a magnificent 4-cam V8 – a GT car boasting supercar performance, with a cleverly styled fastback body by Ghia of Italy. The bodywork rivalled that of the Miura and the Daytona. The Ghibli was the far more attractive sister to its rather clumpy-looking sibling, the Quattroporte. No offence intended.

BELOW ***The Maserati Ghibli. Easy to look at, hard to spell.***

RIGHT ***The Ferrari 365 GTB/4 Daytona Coupe.***

1968 Ferrari Dino An iconic, mid-engined, small Ferrari, the Dino was named after Enzo Ferrari's son, who tragically died in 1956. The Dino is not, strictly speaking, capable of supercar performance – but it has an enduring and stunning silhouette, designed by Pininfarina, that would put most supercar designers to shame. Interestingly, the early models were not badged as Ferrari.

1968 Ferrari 365GTB Daytona Nicknamed the Daytona after a 1-2-3 victory for Ferrari at that famous American track, the Daytona was a replacement for the slow-selling 275GTB/4. It was considered by many to be Ferrari's first overt attempt at building a supercar for road use, as well as a retort to the game-changing Lamborghini Miura. The Daytona was still resolutely front-engined, but nonetheless it had blistering performance, hitting 60mph in just 5.5 seconds and reaching a top speed of 175mph. Sensational lines did not stop some contemporary observers criticising the 'old-fashioned' front-engine layout. Designers Pininfarina said they had discussed a mid-engine layout with Enzo Ferrari – known by his nickname of *The Commendatore* – but he had said 'the horse is in the front of the chariot'. Ferrari had been the last big F1 brand to adopt mid-engines, and in the 1950s Enzo had initially also resisted the onset of disc brake technology. The Daytona's acceleration and top speed both outdid the Miura, making it – for many people – Ferrari's greatest-ever V12.

What about?

Here is a selection of really significant cars that are worthy of further investigation. They might not be game changers, or even the most high-profile cars of their era, but the following vehicles deserve a special mention.

1960 Aston Martin DB4 GT Zagato
1963 Chevrolet Corvette Stingray
1964 Marcos 1800
1965 Ferrari 275GTB
1966 De Tomaso Mangusta
1967 Alfa Romeo Tipo 33 Stradale
1967 Toyota 2000GT (Japan's first ever genuine supercar?)
1968 Marcos Mantis XP
1968 Lamborghini Islero
1971 Lamborghini Espada

Mobilgas
BUSES WELCOME
Mobilgas SPECIAL
Mobilgas
Mobilgas SPECIAL
66

Muscle or Super?

LEFT ***The Chevrolet Corvette: a response to the 'European invasion' of supercars.***

There is a strange contradiction at the heart of America's place in any history of supercars. Despite not being globally renowned for building its own supercars, the United States remains the biggest market for all of the European supercar manufacturers, including Ferrari, Porsche and Lamborghini. America, it seems, loves supercars – it just doesn't build many.

During the course of writing this book, I spoke to one European supercar expert about which US supercars I should include. With a cheeky smile on his face, he simply said, 'Have they actually made any?' He was being a little mischievous, of course, but his is not an altogether lone voice of dissent. Perceived wisdom tells us that American high-performance cars are cumbersome, weighed down by massive engines, poorly built and about as subtle as a sledgehammer on wheels. Some people say they are best reserved for use as straight-line racers – good for the drag strip but unable to handle corners. That rather withering summary is not necessarily this author's opinion, but it is certainly that of many high-performance car experts.

So, if there *are* any American supercars, which models are they and what are they like?

To find out, we first need to take another quick history lesson. European car magazines used the word 'supercar' as long ago as 1910. Fifty years later, and unrelated to this fact, the 'S' word was also widely being used in America to describe a great US automotive icon: the muscle car. There is not enough room here to chronicle the history of muscle cars in any appropriate depth – that would need a separate, very long book! – but I will summarise their story here as they are an important cultural satellite orbiting in the same solar system as Planet Supercar.

First up, a definition: muscle cars are generally deemed to be mid-sized American cars with fierce acceleration and almost always a 'large displacement', meaning they tend to have a pretty huge engine. Typically, we are talking about V8s of 6 litres or more. A muscle car will also, usually, have bodywork that is fairly similar to a related, standard model by the same manufacturer, creating a deceptive balance of relatively 'normal' looks and blistering power. A muscle car's engine is at the front, but the rear wheels drive the beast, ensuring they are great for firing off in a straight line. Muscle cars are also literally 'muscular' in their looks, with their prodigious power almost physically bulging out of the bodywork. Unlike their sleeker European supercar counterparts, muscle cars are also usually relatively affordable to the ordinary wage earner – meaning 'Average Joe' on the street can buy one.

This all sounds rather exhilarating, but there are negatives, too: muscle cars are often berated for their inferior build quality as well as poor handling and bad brakes. This is, perhaps, because the landscape of the USA is so vast that the long cruises necessary across state do not require the finer cornering capabilities of continental performance cars. As for those muscular looks... well, 'subtle they ain't'.

Trans-continental cultural clashes aside, there remains the question of when muscle cars first appeared and, more relevant to this book, whether they can be considered as 'supercars' or not. America has a long and rich history of making high-performance cars. Pre-First World War, exceptional, open two-seater cars such as the Mercer Raceabout and the Stutz Bearcat turned heads, although that sporty, formative genre failed to last. The interwar years marked the first era of the US sedan: larger, more comfortable cars designed to cruise America's elongated highways. In the 1940s and 1950s, post-war America began (though not exclusively) to look to Europe for its performance cars, such as Jaguars, MGs, Ferraris, and Porsches. The Mercedes Gullwing, featured in this book, is a case in point. Home-grown, native, American models tended to have less exotic appeal. The Corvette of 1953 was a response to this European invasion of sorts, with its fibreglass body and 6-cylinder engine, followed by its legendary V8 version two years later. Cars such as the Mustang also helped the cause, but in terms of post-war supercars, America was a little behind the game.

However, what America did produce with aplomb were these so-called muscle cars. The history books offer a number of different dates for these gas-guzzling beasts' Year Zero, with many pointing to the 1964 Pontiac GTO as the inspiration for the genre. However, you can actually go back much further than that.

The 1962 Max Wedge Mopars, for instance, had many of the attributes of a typical muscle car, as did the 1960 Catalina. Or, there is the first production car of 300bhp – the Chrysler 300. Slip back into the 1950s and you will find the quite bulky-looking 1957 Rambler Rebel, seen by many as the first of this new breed of muscle cars (even though it was described as a supercar at the time). *Musclecar Enthusiast* magazine claims this was 'what

some people believe to be the very first muscle car'. The Dodge D-500, also from the late 1950s, was another very early example, as was the Chrysler Hemi from 1951. Going back yet further, the Oldsmobile Rocket 88, from the 1940s, is another candidate for the very first muscle car. The Rocket 88 had a V8 engine, a lighter body than its standard counterpart and – even with just 135bhp – performance that was on a par with almost any rival. The Rocket 88 was entered into NASCAR and won eight of the ten races in which it competed. Muscle car purists will urge you to look back even further – to the mid-1930s and the less-renowned Buick Century from 1936, no less.

The idea of putting a massive engine into a standard-bodied car was itself a throwback to the hot rods of the pre-war era. Along with this illegal drag racing heritage, America's favourite motorsport – NASCAR – played its part in muscle car history, too. The founders of NASCAR would personally seek out cars that offered race-car thrills for a fraction of the price, and heavily customise those models for racing. In doing so, they sparked a revolution that would heavily influence the muscle car culture several decades later.

BELOW ***For many the original muscle car – a Pontiac GTO.***

ABOVE ***A full-sized Oldsmobile 88 from the 1940s.***

While the argument about which was the first muscle car will no doubt rumble on, it is interesting to consider the performance values that a muscle car can offer. With a speed limit of 70mph imposed in most US states by the end of the 1960s, top speeds were not seen as particularly relevant to muscle car enthusiasts (unlike their European supercar counterparts). Instead, acceleration was prioritised, with the established 0–60mph test supplemented with the introduction of the so-called 'quarter-mile' – a standard drag distance found on many American circuits. Some experts suggest that, for any self-respecting muscle car to be ordained as such, it first has to complete a quarter-mile in less than 16 seconds.

The golden age of the muscle car was the 1960s and the early years of the 1970s. The genre's family tree as I see it – as described above – was fairly sparsely populated at first, but by the mid-1960s most manufacturers were climbing onboard the muscle car convoy. There was also a wider cultural sea-change, behind this seismic shift, in how some Americans viewed their daily transportation. President Lyndon Johnson had promised a 'Great Society' when he came to office, and muscle cars were in some ways a part of that. They offered the average person a chance to own a high-performance car and enjoy the subsequent visceral excitement.

The most popular 'classic' muscle car worthy of highlighting is the aforementioned Pontiac GTO from 1964. Pontiac had enjoyed success on the drag strip, and in NASCAR, so all the signs were good. A very famous front cover feature from *Car and Driver* magazine showed the Pontiac GTO racing a red Ferrari GTO, which for many of the mag's readers cemented the American vehicle's place as the first and best muscle car. Many of the parts and technologies used in the GTO were already in existence, but the car was greater than the sum of its parts and became a huge sales hit. The

GTO was stealthy, hiding its enormous power under discreet looks, which only added to the appeal (particularly to those 'faster' drivers who might want to avoid the prying eye of the law). The combination of looks and power proved irresistible. Also, unlike European supercars (this was the era of the Lamborghini Miura), the Pontiac was relatively affordable. The man on the American street was smitten, and the car quickly smashed all manner of sales records. The car's nickname was 'The Goat' and it boasted 335bhp, as well as a 0–60mph time of less than six seconds. However, it was also known for its unreliable brakes and fluffy handling! But no one seemed to mind. Pontiac hoped to sell 5,000 GTOs in the first year. In fact, it sold 32,000. The car went on to sell over 500,000 units in its lifetime. *Motor Trend* magazine wrote, 'the GTO is the leader of the supercars… in image, performance and class… [this is] the car to equal'.

So, 1964 was the year of the Pontiac GTO – but also of the Ford Mustang, which similarly helped to redefine how the American public at large looked at their way of getting around. Mustangs were compact and affordable, sporty and cool. Notably, like so many rival muscle cars, they were not actually marketed as 'muscle cars' at the time. However, when Steve McQueen appeared in one in the 1968 movie *Bullitt*, the Mustang's legend was secured.

BELOW ***The Ford Mustang fastback's silhouette is one of the finest muscle car shapes ever designed. The Ford Mustang GT, driven by Steve McQueen in*** **Bullitt*****, was the very definition of muscle car style.***

Publicity such as this boosted the popularity of the muscle car hugely, and the manufacturers were quick to sniff out a sales opportunity. Actual sales volumes of muscle cars were in fact quite modest, with many high-profile models only selling in the hundreds. However, their PR effect was very powerful. People would often be drawn into showrooms by a high-profile muscle car, only to then buy the standard, more affordable model. This is known in marketing terms as the 'halo effect' – similar in nature to the old adage of 'win on Sunday, sell on Monday' understood by so many racing car manufacturers.

Sometimes, the development of new muscle cars would involve somewhat 'unofficial' tests, with street-racing playing a huge part. There were even whispers of some car designers tacitly engaging illegal street-racers to help them develop new parts. When new, bigger, faster cars were unleashed, some manufacturers resorted to offering cars that had been modified for drag racing, with disclaimers telling the new owners that the cars were not ideal for everyday use.

There followed a golden age of muscle car mania, with ever-more-powerful models being offered. Ordinary members of the public began driving around in huge-engined monsters just to pop to the local store. There are far too many classics to highlight here, but if you are interested you could do worse than look up such beauties as the Dodge Challenger, the Roadrunner, the 1969 Dodge Charger, the 1970 Buick GSX, the 1968 Pontiac Firebird Coupe, the 1970 Boss 302 Mustang, the 1969 Chevy Camaro, the 1968 Plymouth Hemi or the 1970 Chevrolet Chevelle SS 454. This is merely a very small, and debatable, list. There are, of course, many exceptions to the hugely generalised criteria of what constitutes a muscle

BELOW ***1969 Chevrolet Chevelle Yenko Sports car. Flamboyant stripes along the length of the bodywork is a staple of muscle car livery.***

ABOVE **An American institution: the Ford Mustang.**

car. Smaller cars, such as the Chevrolet Nova SS, were very quick. So, too, were many bigger cars such as the Camaro. Some 6-cylinder, turbo-charged US cars might also qualify. Just like the process of describing a supercar, defining a muscle car is a very inexact science.

As mentioned above, during the heyday of the muscle car – in the 1960s and 1970s – the term 'muscle car' was not actually used. Oddly, the cars were more often described as 'supercars'. For example, the Rambler SC had initials that stood for that exact word. The waters are muddied even further by cars such as the Mustang and the Shelby GT500. Since these cars had unique bodies, unrelated to a standard model, they were not even classified by American insurance companies of the day as 'supercars' or 'muscle cars', instead being labelled as 'sporty' or 'pony'.

Then it all started to fade away.

As the 1970s progressed, rising insurance premiums, ever-increasing anti-pollution legislation, the oil crisis of the mid-1970s and a general trend towards greater fuel efficiency and family practicality started to erode the muscle car's appeal. Manufacturers were making increasingly economical cars, and their finance departments started scowling at the muscle cars' ever-decreasing sales figures. The days of the muscle car were numbered.

The first phase of muscle cars ended in the early 1970s, but this great icon of the American auto industry would periodically resurface – both commercially, via major manufacturers, or on the underground, courtesy of tuning companies. There exists a well-established nostalgia market as well as a vogue, within new car manufacturers, for reissuing new versions of old muscle cars.

... And so we come to America's contribution to the subject of this book: supercars. As pointed out above, some historians claim the USA *invented* the term. In the modern era, however, what Europeans tend to call supercars are often qualified as 'exotics' in America. The major brands have occasionally looked at launching supercars – General Motors flirted with the Aerovette and the CERV IV, for example, with limited success. GM also owned Lotus for a time, just as Chrysler owned Lamborghini and Ford had fingers in Aston Martin's pie, but these relationships have never really taken off. In reality, are the above muscle cars really just North American supercars? No, of course not. They are a different breed altogether, designed for a different purpose, appealing to a different psyche and offering an altogether different experience. Which one you prefer is entirely personal, but they are clearly very separate entities.

However, there have been a number of independent US supercar brands of note. The brilliant Vector was hugely promising, but ultimately fell away. DeLorean tried to launch an American supercar brand but also attracted headlines for the wrong reasons (more on this later). However, there are undeniably a number of American 'supercars' that are worthy of note in any book of this kind. Whether they should actually be called 'muscle cars' or 'high-performance cars' or 'super sports cars' can be a conversation for another time.

Callaway C12

The Callaway is a long-nosed, hugely powerful beast similar to the Dodge Viper. Its founder, Reeves Callaway, had previously modified BMW 3-Series models to great effect, so he knew the secrets of high performance. He was particularly renowned for his use of turbos, which was also on show in the work he completed on Alfa Romeos and modified Corvettes. It is the latter car that provided the skeleton for the C12, though this is no Corvette with a body kit. Ingenious additions such as new suspension, larger brakes, better shocks, and custom bodywork mark this car out distinctly as a Callaway. The Corvette V8 is heavily retuned, with its capacity increased and its power output substantially improved. Interior modifications, such as the bucket seats by Koenig, complete the elite look.

Saleen S7

Former racing driver Steve Saleen modified Mustangs for almost two decades before deciding to launch his own mid-engined supercar, the Saleen S7 – a genuine American supercar – in 2000. The S7 certainly had exotic looks, with an aggressive stance and low-slung poise all of its own. Built just south of Los Angeles, the Saleen was an impressive beast. At its launch, the car was heralded as the 'world's fastest production car'. Saleen had earlier built the

GT40 for Ford so the portents were promising. Saleen's modification business continued apace, too, with comedian Tim Allen – voice of Buzz Lightyear – helping to promote some of the company's Mustang conversions. How can you not like a car that Buzz Lightyear wants you to buy?

At only 41 inches high, the Saleen S7 was almost as low-slung as the legendary GT40, and nearly 3 inches lower than a Lamborghini Diablo. The car has a world-record number of 'gills' on its sleek, carbon-fibre bodywork. The '7' in the name stands for the seven litres of the engine's capacity, which is partly comprised of elements from Ford's racing programme. Weight-saving measures such as tubular frames and honeycomb aluminium panels make this car more than 600lb lighter than a Diablo, too, hence the 0–60mph time of less than 4 seconds and the 200mph-plus top speed. The car has the supercar essential of scissor doors, and once in the cabin – although not exactly central, as in the McLaren F1 – the asymmetrical driver's position is more centred than usual. The lack of a rear-view mirror is deliberate, replaced instead with a video camera and screen. Many people think the Saleen is the closest thing to a GT race car fitted for the road, yet it has air-conditioning, luxury leather upholstery, watch-face gauges, electric windows, and a brilliant sound system. The later S7 models were ludicrously fast – achieving 0–60mph in 2.7 seconds and with top speeds in excess of 235mph. These impressive stats put it in Bugatti

BELOW ***Anyone who says that America doesn't make supercars needs to check out this Saleen!***

Veyron and McLaren F1 territory, while the twin turbo top-of-the-range model had a whopping 750bhp.

With such brutal power and Steve Saleen's own vast racing experience, it was no surprise that Saleens faired exceptionally well on the race track alongside the cars of companies many times larger. Saleen won their class at the 12 Hours of Sebring and performed very well at Le Mans, as well as winning multiple international championships. This pedigree has inspired Saleen to adopt its own unique racing colour, 'liztick red', which was named in honour of Steve's wife, Elizabeth. Although the company has endured some difficult corporate restructuring over the years, in 2012 Steve Saleen was reunited with the Saleen brand, for what may well prove to be a very exciting future.

Dodge Viper

The Dodge Viper is perhaps the one US car that should be credited with being, to some degree, a game changer in the world of supercars. This is not because it had the most advanced engine ever produced or the most muscular looks, or indeed the quickest sprint time but because, in a sense, it disproved many of the misconceptions about American muscle cars that were found around the globe. They were accused of being heavy, having poor handling and bad brakes, and of being no good for the race track – only the drag racing scene. Not so the Viper.

RIGHT ***The Dodge Viper went a long way towards dispelling the negative myths about muscle cars' handling and racing prowess, proving to be a big success on both road and track.***

The front-engined, rear-wheel-driven car was a deliberate statement of intent from Dodge. The aim was to 'jazz up' the Dodge division of the Chrysler car company, and so a plan was drawn up to create something exceptionally powerful that continued the USA's rich muscle car history, but for a new era. The car debuted at the Detroit Auto Show in 1989, as a concept, and proved so popular that a production run was instantly commissioned. Part of the car's development was openly influenced by the Cobra 427, with Carroll Shelby involved in the car's evolution. (Various hints of the AC Cobra can be identified in the Viper, such as the exhaust's side positioning.) Fibreglass bodywork and a tubular steel chassis completed a strong concept. In classic muscle car style, when the concept car was replaced by the eventual production car, the power output had actually increased from 300bhp to 400bhp.

On its launch, the Viper boasted the biggest production engine in the world, a colossal 7,998cc (developed in conjunction with Lamborghini). For the SRT-10 variant of the Viper, Dodge essentially took the 8.4-litre, 10-cylinder, 400bhp-plus engine out of a Chrysler LA truck, remade it in aluminium and crammed it under the bonnet. The Viper's V10 was an engine set-up that was widely used in Formula 1 at the time, but which was highly unusual in road cars. As a result, the engine sound of the Viper has to be heard to be believed. The engine block is very long, housing the V10 that made such a fabulous racket. The car was affordable, too, like all great muscle cars. Critics pointed to the cockpit getting too hot on summer days, the poor build quality of some early models, the poor handling and so on... the usual muscle car problems. Again, no one seemed to care.

The GTS-R race variant of the Dodge Viper was an obvious next step, not least because the Viper was always intended as a no-frills car, lacking as it did many electronic driver aids and modern gadgetry. It has performed with huge success at races such as the GT2 class at Le Mans (finishing first and second in 1997/8) and the 24-Hours Nürburgring event. It also became the first American car to win the overall GT2 World Championship, which it achieved three times in succession and five times overall. The Viper also won the hugely prestigious 24 Hours of Daytona. It is this impressive and versatile racing pedigree that earns the Viper its status as possibly the most influential American car within the supercar lexicon. The Viper is the only modern US car that is seriously able to challenge the stature of the Corvette – although it must be said that the Corvette's most modern incarnations have also enjoyed considerable track success, not least at Le Mans.

The Viper is the American equivalent of the Lamborghini Countach or the Ferrari F40 – the stuff of fantasy. If you were to give an American kid a pencil or crayon he would most likely draw a Dodge Viper. The Viper was, and will always remain, an *homage* to brute horsepower.

SUPERCAR FACT
Dodge built ten Tomahawk motorbikes using a version of the same truck engine found in the Viper. These bonkers bikes were essentially a massive, modified truck engine with two wheels shunted onto each end.

SUPERCAR FACT
Muscle car mania has spread across the globe. Australia has its own rich subculture of such cars, with brands such as Holden applying a uniquely Antipodean approach to the idea.

The 1970s

LEFT ***The era-defining Lamborghini Countach in the background, behind a genuine global TV star – Magnum PI's beauty, the stunning Ferrari 308GTB.***

As the 1960s ended, the Lamborghini Miura and the Ferrari Dino were the only notable mid-engined 'modern' supercar layouts in existence. By contrast, the 1970s would prove to be a very fruitful decade for this supercar breed, despite the severe economic crisis of the time that threatened the very existence of high-performance cars.

As the 1970s started, the world fell in love with compact family cars and also with a new range of 4x4s. However, regardless of drivers' budgets, the Fuel Crisis of 1973 posed a big threat to car lovers everywhere. Beginning in October, an embargo was declared by oil producers embroiled in complex political and strategic confrontations against the USA, the UK, and parts of Europe. The result was that those territories suffered chronic fuel shortages and rocketing prices (in some countries pump prices quadrupled) until March 1974.

The fears sparked by both the protracted fuel crisis and a global recession, following the stock market crash of 1973–74, led to panic across virtually all areas of the consumer world. Supercars were especially vulnerable and many of the smaller sports car companies simply could not survive. Bankruptcies were widespread.

Another factor was the fact that the USA imposed a 55mph speed limit – a speed that many supercars could reach in first gear – plus increasingly strict emissions and safety legislation. So there was a sense that, on paper at least, the supercar might be approaching the end of its days. Such extravagant cars now seemed destined for extinction.

If you were a supercar maker in the early 1970s, you might have been forgiven for throwing in the towel and starting to make family hatchbacks.

Instead, something else happened. In among all this doom and gloom, Lamborghini did what it does best – it launched what some now consider to be the most incredible supercar ever built, the completely bonkers Countach. This was the first, and maddest, in a long line of futuristic 1970s supercars.

The decade also saw a growing distance between race cars and road cars. Racers were now easily capable of 200mph, or more, and looked less and less like a normal car with every passing year. However, this didn't stop supercar makers pushing on with ever faster and more extravagant designs. The Countach is perhaps the most obvious example of this breed, but the so-called 'wedge' shape that it took came to typify the 1970s supercar. Motor shows all around the world displayed these automotive wedges, so that for a while it seemed that everyone was getting in on the act. Take, for instance, the mad concept cars such as the Alfa Romeo Navajo, in 1976, or the Vauxhall SRV of 1970. Supercars also found themselves appearing in movies and TV shows. So, instead of hiding away amidst the chaos, the supercar reacted to the threat of the 1970s by becoming even more extreme, even more visually exotic, and even more flamboyant. Perhaps the depressing oil crisis and all those economic worries just made the escapism of a fantastical supercar all the more appealing...

BELOW **The Ferrari 365 GT4/BB.**

1973 Ferrari Berlinetta Boxer 365 GT4/BB

The 4.4-litre, flat-12 Berlinetta Boxer was essentially Ferrari's belated reply to Lamborghini's game-changing Miura. Here, finally, was a mid-engined Ferrari that would be the marque's most powerful car, using the same horizontal piston layout as the 911. Ferrari had, in fact, been using flat-12s in their race cars since 1964; it was only in their road cars that they hadn't yet made the leap of faith. The Boxer coincided with Ferrari's Grand Prix comeback of the 1970s, reminding us all that this was a racing breed.

The Boxer first appeared at the Turin Motor Show as a concept car in 1971 (although a 1968 show car had many similarities), and suffered somewhat for appearing in the wake of the outrageous Lamborghini Countach concept, seen at Geneva a few months earlier. The Boxer took a more suave approach to design lines than its extravagant rival, and the Ferrari was actually first to go into production, in 1973, one year before the famous Lamborghini. The Boxer was designed by Leonardo Fioravanti, who had previously created the Daytona in his twenties, and who also worked on the Dino and later the fabulous 308GTB (to which you can see a family resemblance). Among the technology Fioravanti utilised was one of Europe's first wind tunnels, located at the company he worked for, Pininfarina. The Boxer has hints of the later 288GTO in its lines, although it is less muscular (but no less dramatic). The body was a mix of steel and aluminium panels, set over a steel tubing frame. Surprisingly, the fantastic looks were not especially aero-efficient, with the car carrying a worse coefficient of drag than a Ford Sierra. The exotic exterior was mixed with the surprisingly plain interior – the sun visors were simply roll-ups and were held in place with suction cups.

The engine was not revolutionary but the car had some interesting elements – for example, because the engine was so long, the gearbox had to be mounted below the engine, rather than in line with it. Some critics suggested that this compromised the centre of gravity and therefore the performance. Although Ferrari had been late to the game, the Boxer set a pattern that would be followed by a generation of Ferraris thereafter. Later versions were more refined and easier to drive, but retained the great level of performance. Even though the Boxer was slower than the outgoing Daytona, it was still one of the world's fastest cars, and its sleek lines and street presence made it a huge hit. The Boxer remains, to this day, one of the all-time great Ferrari silhouettes.

1973 Maserati Bora

This was the first mid-engined production Maserati, launched as a retort to the incredible Miura, and following on from the Italian company's Ghibli. Maserati used a mid-mounted, 4.7-litre V8 engine that was detuned from the Ghibli, which generated 300bhp and had a decidedly American exhaust sound. The engine had previously been used in an almost identical form in numerous race cars such as the 450S.

For many years Maserati was, in fact, better known in the USA than Ferrari. The history books date the Maserati brothers' first race cars back to 1926, after which they enjoyed success for the next decade. With German cars dominating the F1 circuit in the decades immediately afterwards, Maserati moved into American circuit racing, although Fangio did win the F1 title in a Maserati in 1957, so the pedigree was clearly there. Their revolutionary 'Birdcage' racing cars of the early 1960s had also been a high point for the marque.

In 1968, Maserati was sold to Citroën and the Bora was the first result of the French brand's efforts to capture a slice of the mid-engined supercar market. Italdesign's Giorgetto Giugiaro oversaw the car, and he was keen to make a sleek silhouette that did not have 'unnecessary decorations'.

There was some intriguing innovation – Citroën brought its reputation for hydraulic know-how to an innovative brake system, as well as by introducing pedals that moved forwards and backwards, allowing the car to be driven by a person of almost any size. Although not as extravagant as the Miura, one design feature of note was the brushed stainless steel roof and windscreen pillars – a finish later seen on the DeLorean.

On the negative side, the car was heavy and took a steady 7.2 seconds to get to 60mph, plus some testers said that, when driving, it was easy to lose the back end. And it was also thirsty, sometimes not even reaching double figures in mpg. The year 1971 had been a big one for Italian mid-engined supercars – the Countach had launched at Geneva and stunned the world, people were wondering how long Ferrari would take to respond – and lost in the crossfire, somewhat, was the Bora. Reviewers used words like 'practical' and 'restful' to describe the car, and this wasn't exactly awe-inspiring – especially when the Countach was in town. Conversely, however, CAR magazine called it 'one of the finest fast cars ever built.' You decide.

RIGHT ***A Maserati Bora taking some sea air. It's off to get an ice cream in a minute.***

GAME CHANGER

1974 Lamborghini Countach

ABOVE ***The Lamborghini Countach. The name is pronounced 'coon-tash,' not 'count-ash'.***

IF YOU ASK AN ENTIRE GENERATION OF SUPERCAR FANS that grew up in the 1970s and 1980s which car they had as a poster on their wall, you can guarantee that a majority will answer: the Lamborghini Countach. Perhaps more than any other supercar, the Countach has a look that is so startling, so extreme and so distinctive that even in the 21st century, decades after its launch, it is still right up there in any list of all-time great supercars.

My own experience with the Countach is perhaps typical of why the car made such a massive impact. I was on a primary school trip to London as an 11-year-old, excitedly but wearily walking around museums, the

LEFT ***Alfa Romeo Carabo – a secret supercar legend? Meaning 'beetle', the Carabo was an amazing predecessor to the Countach. This concept car was built by Gandini when at Bertone in 1968. Sitting on an Alfa Romeo racing car chassis (the Tipo 33), with an extremely low and very angular body, the Carabo's hinged upright scissor doors were a world first. There are visible hints of the Porsche 917, which also influenced the Countach, and Gandini himself acknowledged the influence of the Lola T70 Coupe.***

SUPERCAR FACT
There is a LEGO version of the Countach, perhaps the ultimate nostalgia trip for 1980s fans.

Embankment and, finally, in the hunt for some tourist food, taking a stroll through Covent Garden. And that was when I saw it. Parked up opposite the Tube station was a crisp white Lamborghini Countach.

An expensively dressed man had the scissor door raised up and was sitting on the sill of the Lambo, leaning out of the car, looking over his shoulder and parallel parking the Countach perfectly into a tight space. An excitable crowd had gathered around, taking photos. As an adult, I would come to realise this parking manoeuvre was no mean feat, especially under such a public spotlight. At the time it was, quite simply, the most astonishing thing my young eyes had ever seen. If my eyeballs could have come out of my head, in the style of *Tom and Jerry*, they would have. I remember the feeling as if it was yesterday, it was just so *exciting*. All of my mates stared, too. Everywhere in the street people were chattering and taking photos. If an alien spaceship had landed just at that moment and announced the Earth was now a colony of Mars, no one would have been listening. The car was so futuristic that, when the man locked the door and simply walked away, I was almost surprised he hadn't zoomed off on a hover-board or teleported himself to his next meeting. (Of course, I realised later why he hadn't used a hover-board – it wouldn't have fitted into the very limited luggage space in the Countach.) From that moment on, the Countach was imprinted on my brain and soul.

How were Lamborghini able to do this? How did they create a car – just a shaped chunk of metal on four bits of rubber – that drew such an emotional reaction from millions of people around the world? It is time for a little more supercar history...

The Countach was designed by the same genius who had been involved in the creation of the Miura: Marcello Gandini of the Bertone design house. In 1971, Gandini stunned the world by unveiling a bright yellow concept Countach at the Geneva Motor Show. Various stunning supercar concepts had appeared at motor shows in the late 1960s, but Lamborghini wanted to make this particular concept a reality. Known internally as Project 112, the Countach stole a march on all its rivals, most notably Ferrari's much-heralded 365GT-BB. Remarkably, some reports suggested that the new, shorter-wheel-base car was so breathtaking that some show-goers didn't even notice the updated Miura SV, also on the stand that day. Given that some car experts had doubted how anyone could possibly follow the legendary Miura with any success, this was impressive. The press reaction was similarly dazzled. On its retail launch, *CAR* magazine said, 'The Countach breathes naked aggression from every pore'. Gandini himself said he wanted, 'People to be astonished when they saw the car'. He would not be disappointed.

One of the most immediate impressions you get of the Countach up close is how low it is. This incredibly low-slung car – approximately 42 inches high – was centred around dozens of trapezoidal design motifs, an idea that would be replicated in the hexagon-obsessed Aventador and after that the Huracán. As such, the Countach is an explosion of non-organic creases and folds. Gandini's trademark asymmetric wheel arches added to the unique look, sitting above a very early example of alloy wheels.

Add to that the scissor doors – what else? – as well as entirely futuristic lines and it is clear why this stunning car looked like nothing the world had ever seen. 'It just blew everybody away when it was launched,' recounts Lamborghini UK's legendary salesman Steve Higgins. Notably, in a reversal

BELOW ***The story goes that when designer Marcello Gandini first showed the concept car to a reporter friend of his, the pal uttered the word 'Countach!', which is a (non-obscene) expletive in the Piedmontese dialect of Italian, uttered when a man sees a very beautiful woman.***

of the usual pattern of toning down concept cars for their commercial version, the early production Countachs were, if anything, even more aggressively styled than their concept predecessors, with larger air scoops and bigger vents. Another point of interest regarding the aesthetics of Countach owners, is that when Lamborghini later made a rear wing option available, to make the car look even more outrageous, the vast majority of buyers opted instead for the spoiler.

The car's aggressive look was not just an aesthetic indulgence, though; the NACA ducts were in place for very specific cooling purposes, even though the large rear vent was responsible for eating up almost all of the driver's rear-view. The truly space-age bodywork was made from aircraft-grade aluminium, a method most commonly found in racing cars of the day. Underneath, an innovative tubular space-frame provided the skeleton.

The Countach was powered by a mid-engined V12, mounted longitudinally rather than transversely, as the Miura was. (Early models actually used a Miura 4-litre power plant.) The driver's close proximity to the V12 made for an operatic experience inside the tiny cabin. And the Countach was no slouch, being the fastest road car on its launch, with a top speed of 183mph.

Due to the gearbox sitting in front of the engine, driver and passenger were separated by a huge, central console that housed the transmission. The gear stick plugged directly into the gearbox and, when driving, the whine of the auxiliary oil pump serving the gearbox could be clearly heard.

The driving position was almost horizontal, once again aping racing cars of the day. One contemporary writer likened it to lying in the bottom of a lightbulb. Such gripes about interior build quality were often attributed to the fact that Lamborghini was still a modest-sized supercar player, with the cars essentially hand-built – no robots involved – at a rate of just three a week. The minimalist interior consisted of painted aluminium, leather and pretty much nothing else. While the Miura sometimes suffered from front-end lift at high speeds, the Countach hugged the ground far more tightly, making the long nose of the car pretty much invisible to the driver. The way the windshield followed the exact angle of the nose of the car was also an industry first. Pop-up headlights helped to preserve these sleek lines.

RIGHT ***Has there ever been a more outlandish supercar than the Lamborghini Countach?***

BELOW ***The Countach's incredible looks sometimes overshadowed its mechanical pedigree. The V12 power plant made the cabin inside a Countach not a place for people with sensitive ears!***

This expanse of windscreen made the interior cabin a sweltering greenhouse in sunshine, even with the addition of air-conditioning (there was no stereo, incidentally). There was one, insect-like, spindly pantograph windscreen wiper that was reputed to lift off the glass at speeds in excess of 120mph on some models. But, then, if you are doing that speed in a Lamborghini Countach in the pouring rain, you will have far more urgent things to worry about (not least given the brakes are smaller than those on a modern Renault Clio RS).

Over the car's lengthy 16-year, 2,000-plus car production run, the engine and also the bodywork were regularly tweaked and upgraded. Later models were embellished with fins and body parts, to the disdain of some purists. However, the (undoubtedly fine) engineering is not really what the car is best remembered for. 'As far as the drive is concerned,' explains Lamborghini's

F924 OYR

Steve Higgins, 'like all of these older cars, the Countach was challenging! The interior is quite cramped, the rear vision is minimal, it's not a car that you jump in to go cruising up and down the road. You have got to really mean it and want to do it when you get in a Countach. It is noisy and hot, with a heavy clutch and stiff gear shift. But, really, look at it – do you care?'

Countach owners were, by definition, bold, extravagant people. One Japanese car collector actually commissioned a new house to be designed with a central car elevator that could lift his Countach (and other cars) right into his living room – final proof, if needed, that the design lines are as much art as they are automotive.

There were, of course, practical limitations galore. If you take a Countach to a McDonald's drive-in, you can fit a quarter-pounder through the tiny non-electric side-window slits, but not a Big Mac! This was not a car for the frugal, either. At a time when fuel rationing was on the cards, in the middle of the 1970s, the Countach represented perhaps the ultimate motoring extravagance. (Driven 'heartily' you would be lucky to see double figures in mpg.)

ABOVE ***Ferruccio Lamborghini had his own red Countach repainted in white, because he thought that was the car's best colour.***

RIGHT ***Scissors doors, outrageous looks, bright paintwork, massive engine, breathtaking performance? I give you the Lamborghini Countach.***

The Countach is now established as one of the all-time great supercars. But is it a game changer? Undeniably, yes. During its active lifetime, chiefly in the 1980s, the car played an important role in keeping a financially struggling Lamborghini at the forefront of all supercar fanatics' minds. (Ferruccio had sold his shares three years before the Countach was launched.) It is also a fact that the Countach is a truly global icon. When the Australian International Concourse d'Elegance Show advertised its 2013 event, it did so with a painting of a Countach adorning the front of the programme. Perhaps the last word is best left to a man who knows the Countach better than most, Steve Higgins of Lamborghini: 'What surprises me is that the Countach remains current to this day – so many guys walk in here and say they had that famous poster of a red Countach on the wall when they were a kid. It's amazing how many buyers still mention it. In many ways, I would say that it is probably *the* iconic supercar design of all time.'

Lamborghini Countach
LAUNCHED
1974
POWER
375bhp
ACCELERATION
0–60mph in 5.4 secs
MAXIMUM SPEED
192mph
PRODUCTION RUN
2000-plus cars were produced over 16 years

1975 Porsche 911 Turbo

Porsche created a performance car legend with the lightweight 911 2.7 RS of 1972. The extreme RSR variant followed, and then – in 1974–75 – they did it again. With horsepower limitations having to be introduced in some racing formulas, to stop cars from literally taking off, manufacturers were using smaller engines fitted with turbos to create a better performance. In 1975 Porsche fitted one of these new engines to their iconic 911 and a legend was reborn. That the Turbo also came with huge spoilers and wide, flared wheel arches added sensational looks to the car's enhanced performance, and set a precedent for future supercar silhouettes. Dreadful turbo lag, shocking levels of oversteer and only four gears made this perhaps the world's scariest supercar to drive. To this day, the 1975 911 Turbo remains one of *the* iconic supercars.

1976 Lotus Esprit

If a supercar's impact is to be judged on its profile and global celebrity, then the Lotus Esprit is in the upper echelons of the breed. The Esprit does not owe its status primarily to its stellar performance, revolutionary technology, or landmark design – but rather to the fact that James Bond turned the car into a submarine in the 1977 blockbuster movie, *The Spy Who Loved Me*.

Before Mr Bond turned the Esprit into an overnight sensation, the car had enjoyed a welcome, albeit modest, introduction to the supercar world. On its launch, in 1975, it had only a sloped 4-cylinder, 156bhp engine, which caused some to doubt whether it was a supercar at all. The final production car was very similar to a striking 1972 concept, but with a less raked screen. The body was built as top and bottom halves, which is why you can see a join line running along the length of the car. The stunning angular looks came at the expense of rear visibility, which was very poor, while the car's width was huge.

BELOW ***The Porsche 911 Turbo reinvented a supercar legend, and is a design and cultural icon of the 1970s.***

ABOVE ***James Bond's legendary 'submarine' Esprit. The original name of 'Lotus Kiwi' was shunned for 'Esprit', as all Lotus cars begin with the letter 'e'. Two Esprit Turbos later appeared in the 1981 Bond movie,*** **For Your Eyes Only.**

Fortunately, the founder of Lotus – Colin Chapman – had a mantra of 'speed through lightness', so, despite its size, the car only weighed around 1,000kg. Nonetheless, many testers of early versions of the car criticised the awkward gear changes and lack of power. The second of those complaints was one that would haunt the Esprit for much of the earlier stages of its life. These gripes stopped in 1980, when Lotus launched a Turbo version at the Royal Albert Hall, in London, with a jazzy party. Resplendent with NACA ducts in the bonnet, spoilers and side skirting, the first 100 cars were painted in the red and blue livery of Lotus's F1 sponsor, Essex Petroleum. This was Lotus's fastest road car ever – by some stretch.

The bodywork was styled by designer Giorgetto Giugiaro. It was one of several 'folded paper' designs he had been working on. Independent suspension at the front and rear, and a so-called 'backbone chassis' – typical of Lotus – were also noteworthy. The car had a fibreglass body that was said by some to smell of glue, adding to general quibbles about build quality. Like all Lotus cars, it handled brilliantly. With Mario Andretti winning the 1978 F1 World Championship in a Lotus, too, the marque's name was on everyone's lips.

However appealing it might have been, though, the Esprit of the 1970s was not about to outperform most supercars in terms of performance. That said, no one cared because James Bond had a white one that turned into a submarine. Movie legend tells us that Lotus PR man Donovan McLauchlan had heard of a new Bond movie being filmed at Pinewood Studios, and so he took a pre-production Esprit to the studio lot and parked it in a place where anyone entering would have to walk past it. Bond director Cubby Broccoli saw the car, and the rest is history...

Bond's Esprit became the most famous supercar in the world, overnight, when it appeared as a submarine-car in *The Spy Who Loved*

ABOVE ***This Esprit (pictured) was made for Lotus founder Colin Chapman. It includes special features such as specific pollen filters (apparently Colin Chapman suffered from bad hay fever), an early form of power steering, and numerous aerodynamic changes.***

Me. After driving off a pier and plunging into the sea, the Esprit transforms into an underwater war machine, complete with anti-aircraft missiles, a periscope, mines, a smoke screen, and rocket launchers. The car eventually drives up onto a beach on its way to take part in more espionage adventures. Millions of kids (and their dads) around the world suddenly wanted a Lotus Esprit – or at least a die-cast model of one.

Amazingly, the actual Bond car used in the film works as a submarine, but not as a car. It has four propellers driven by electric motors in waterproof chambers. The fins can actually be operated by the driver. The turning circle underwater is 20 feet, and its dive and climb performance are controlled by ballast tanks. Made by Perry Oceanographics, especially for the movie, it reputedly cost over $100,000 to build, used up five Esprit body shells, and was driven by a retired Navy Seal during the underwater scenes.

Following the success of the Bond movie, Lotus announced that the Esprit now carried a three-year waiting list. Such was the car's appeal, there began a period when Esprit posters replaced Countachs on a million bedroom walls. In this sense, the Esprit was a game changer, but not necessarily for its performance or engineering – perharps mainly for its persona and cultural impact.

The vehicle used in the film – dubbed 'Wet Nellie' – sold at auction in 2013 for more than £600,000 ($1 million) to the founder of Tesla electric road cars, Elon Musk. He told the press that he had watched the Bond movie as a kid and that it was a dream to get hold of that actual car (he plans to insert a Tesla motor into it). This was not the Esprit's only big screen appearance. A Stevens Esprit appeared in *Pretty Woman,* allegedly after Ferrari and Porsche declined to be involved due to the storyline involving a prostitute. Lotus Esprit sales tripled over the next two years. The Esprit has also featured in *Basic Instinct, The Rookie, Taking Care of Business, If Looks Could Kill: Teen Agent,* and the TV series *The Highwayman.*

Eventually, however, even the glitter of the silver screen couldn't stop the Esprit from looking dated. Updates were required. The 1980 Turbo edition finally gave the Esprit the power it deserved, while later limited editions, such as the 3.5-litre V8, kept the car alive for another few years. Exterior redesigns, courtesy of Peter Stevens – who later designed the McLaren F1 – kept the spirit alive while all-aluminium bodies and numerous power boosts helped to add to the legend. The final 350 version, of 1999, offered stunning pace. This longevity led one car writer to brand the Esprit the 'evergreen geriatric' of the supercar world. When the car was eventually retired to the great supercar garage in the sky, it was over three decades old and had sold 10,000 units since that famous Turin concept car. In that sense it is an anomaly: a car that has lasted almost three decades in a world where three years is a lifetime... Must have been all that sea air.

1978 BMW M1

The 1978 M1 is the German marque's only entry in this supercar book. Like the Porsche 959 of a decade later, the 3.5-litre, straight-6-engined M1 attempted to utilize the latest cutting-edge technology, this time to create a car for Group 5 competitions – a Touring Car-style racing formula, initially with a 5-litre engine limit. The M1 had many supercar traits – it was mid-engined, Italian (with a Lamborghini-built steel tube chassis), had a fibreglass body, a well made but slightly cramped interior, and bodywork designed by Giugiaro (an earlier gullwing concept version did not make it to production). For all that, however, the M1 struggled in motorsport competitions against rivals such as Porsche, and it underperformed commercially, ultimately costing BMW a lot of money. Although BMW is not known for purist supercars, the M1 – with its superb handling – was the forefather of the marque's famously high-performance M series of cars, with a similar engine ending up in the very first M5.

BELOW **The BMW M1.**

Also in the 1970s

1970 Mercedes Benz C111 Initially intended to race at Le Mans, fifty units were planned but only six were ever built. Gullwinged like its Grandaddy, the 300 SL, the C111's pitiful fuel consumption was rumoured to be in single figures.

1970 Citroën SM After Citroën purchased Maserati, it launched the Bora as well as the SM, a V6, front-wheel-drive supercar with pneumatic suspension. The large rear window and oddly squared rear end was very Gallic and distinctive.

BELOW **A Lamborghini Urraco in Wales.**

ABOVE **One of the all-time most underrated supercars – the De Tomaso Pantera.**

1970 Lamborghini Urraco A more modest, mid-engined brother to the wonderful Miura, the V8 Urraco never captured the imagination in the same way as its sibling. It cost Lamborghini a small fortune to develop, and although it was faster than a Dino, the Urraco sold only modestly. Once the Countach arrived, it was all over anyway!

1971 De Tomaso Pantera The De Tomaso Pantera was a very angular supercar, housing a Ford V8 underneath a futuristic body styled by Ghia. Hand-built in limited numbers, with a reputation for unreliability, Elvis Presley is alleged to have shot his car with a pistol out of frustration. This was a stunning supercar, nonetheless.

1971 Alpine A310 The A310 was based on rally-winning cars, with a lightweight fibreglass body and with angular, sporty looks. It had a rear-engined layout, however.

1973 Ferrari 512BB The Boxer was superceded by the 512BB in 1976, which, for many, boasts the definitive 1970s supercar look.

1973 Lancia Stratos Originally conceived as just a styling project, the Stratos's lines were so spectacular that they inspired Lancia to actually build the car. Styled by Bertone – using the Ferrari Dino's 2.4-litre, V6, mid-mounted power train – the car was a rally sensation. Lancia also built road-going examples of this ultra-lightweight, plastic-bodied car that were blisteringly quick. The wrap-around windscreen, short wheel base and superb body aerodynamics make this tiny machine one of the greatest rally cars of all time. A new version was launched in 2010.

1977 Panther 6 Only two examples of the 1977 Panther 6 were ever made, so it may not qualify as a production car. However, the 8.2-litre, twin-turbo-charged six-wheeler was alleged to have topped 200mph – which, if verified, would have made it the first ever road car to do so.

1977 Aston Martin V8 Vantage The Vantage created vast amounts of power, with a macho 5.3-litre engine – barely kept in check by some pretty ordinary handling – which was claimed to deliver a world-beating top speed

BELOW RIGHT ***The Ferrari 308GTS, made famous by Magnum PI. Similar to the James Bond Lotus Esprit, the celebrity association of being regularly seen on TV made this car one of the highest-profile Ferraris ever.***

BELOW ***The Lancia Stratos was a rallying legend. However, it did have such a small cabin that, for all but the daintiest of passengers, was quite cramped. Pictured here is a meticulous replica.***

of 170mph when it was launched. Aston gave no specific bhp figure, instead saying only that the power output was 'adequate'. The Vantage was once clocked to have wheel spun for 80 feet.

1978 Ferrari 308GTS One of the most beautiful Ferraris ever made, the 308GTS was made famous by the moustache-ioed private investigator, Magnum PI, whose TV series became a worldwide smash. The 3-litre V8 was mid-mounted. Designed to replace the Dino 246, early examples had an entirely glass-reinforced plastic lightweight body. The 308GTS had super handling and a fierce engine, but it was the gorgeous styling that made the car stand out. Magnum PI's car was auctioned off at the end of each series.

1979 Aston Martin Bulldog The Bulldog was Aston's first mid-engined supercar, complete with scissor doors, a height of just 43 inches, and a rumoured top speed of over 200mph. Sadly, although the plan was to make 25 units, financial problems meant that only one concept car was made – which nonetheless clocked up 191mph.

What about?

Here is a selection of really significant cars that are worthy of further investigation. They might not be game changers, or even the most high-profile cars of their era, but the following vehicles deserve special mention.

1970 Monteverdi Hai

1973 Matra-Simca Bagheera

1973 Caterham 7

1971 Aston Martin DBS V8 (Did a 160mph, high-speed run on a not-as-yet finished part of the M4 motorway.)

1975 Dome Zero (Possibly the maddest-looking 'wedge' car ever.)

1977 Vector W8

The 1980s

LEFT The stunning Ferrari 288GTO: one of the most influential and pivotal supercars ever made.

The 1980s was a period of odd contrasts for the supercar. The buoyant global economy put money in the pockets of millions of people – most famously, perhaps, creating so-called 'yuppies', newly rich financiers proud of their conspicuous consumption, yet laughed at by serious petrol-heads as self-indulgent and ill-informed buyers of supercars. At the opposite end of the spectrum, the raw and ultimately lethal Group B rallying formula – easily worthy of a book on its own – spawned a number of brutally fast, stripped-out cars which would inform the new generation of supercars.

The rise of the computer started to filter into car technology, too. And the 1980s was also the decade of the turbocharger, with first race cars, then supercars – and ultimately, road cars – all utilising the performance-boosting technology. Incidentally, by the end of the 1980s, these turbos had become so powerful that legislation was introduced to limit their output and, as a result, normally aspirated engines came back into fashion.

It wasn't just supercars that were making the headlines, however. The watershed Audi Quattro, for instance, introduced four-wheel drive and revolutionised rallying and – in turn – the wider car world. At the same time, cars such as the Sierra Cosworth and Peugeot 205GTI were making high-speed driving more affordable for the everyday driver, meaning it wasn't just supercars for the wealthy that offered a speed fix anymore.

The 1980s was also a decade that was not particularly kind to British motor manufacturers, with Britain's two main proponents – Aston Martin and Lotus – barely scraping through. By contrast, if any manufacturer can claim to have overpowered its rivals during the 1980s, it is Ferrari, who produced at least two cars of exceptional historical significance, and several more besides. Never write off the Prancing Horse.

1981 DeLorean DMC-12

Just as the later Ferrari 288GTO almost made it into my Top Ten, there is another car that was *almost* included for an entirely unique reason. The DeLorean DMC-12 may not have supercar performance, power or mystique, BUT it was the only car I knew of as a kid that enabled you to travel through time. And it still is, as far as I am aware.

BELOW **The DeLorean looked breathtaking with its gullwing doors opened: a high-profile attempt at making a genuinely British-built supercar.**

ABOVE ***Close-up view of the rear of a DeLorean sports car.***

SUPERCAR FACT
Back to the Future – customer modifications were rare but one American doctor added a flux capacitor, which enabled time travel.

SUPERCAR FACT
Three of the DeLoreans produced were actually plated in 24-carat gold.

The project was the brainchild of John DeLorean, a former leading light at Pontiac. DeLorean's ambitious dream of building a supercar soon attracted celebrity backers as well as a multi-million-pound investment from the British government. The government's backing was used to help DeLorean build a state-of-the-art factory in Northern Ireland at a time when unemployment there was high.

DeLorean had launched a concept car in 1977, which had two very distinctive features – gullwing doors and an unpainted body made from brushed stainless steel. Both of these fabulous supercar features would make it on to the eventual production car. However, both features also presented a problem, as they added weight. DeLorean, though, was insistent that the car should have gullwing doors to increase its appeal (and he was right, as they made the car looks fantastic). And while the steel may have been unusual, it had the advantage that, if you lightly scratched the bodywork, you could simply use a scouring pad to rescue the finish.

The car had no shortage of world experts on board during its development, including Giugiaro, who styled the body during his 'folded paper' era (when he also created the Lotus Esprit). After the concept car had launched, Lotus were brought on board to evolve a steel-backbone chassis. In fact, much of the car's underpinnings were based around the brilliant Esprit. However, a rushed production schedule meant that when the car finally went on sale there were numerous reliability and quality issues, especially on the earlier models. The Renault V6, all-alloy rear-mounted engine generated just 130bhp, so acceleration was modest (0–60mph in 10.5 seconds). A twin-turbo model was planned but, sadly, never made it into production. Handling was decent, if not exceptional. The interior was available in black or grey, and was surprisingly roomy – John DeLorean was 6 feet 4 inches, so he made sure it was welcoming for tall people.

However, for all its shortcomings... of all the supercars in this book, the DeLorean is absolutely on a par with the very best in terms of the cultural impact it made. This, of course, is because it featured in the highest-grossing film of 1985, *Back to the Future*, starring Michael J. Fox. In the movie, madcap scientist Dr Emmett L. Brown uses a DeLorean fitted with a flux capacitor to travel through time.

Unfortunately, financial difficulties saw the car ultimately fail to deliver on its early promise and the whole project eventually collapsed. Fortunately, however, a company based in Texas, USA, consisting of world experts on the car, has continued the legend. They have been building DeLoreans with painstaking attention to detail, using original parts and original vehicle identification numbers, thus securing the future of this supercar icon.

To my mind, as a child of the mid-1980s, the DeLorean was without doubt one of the greatest ever supercars, along with the James Bond submarine Esprit of the decade before. I am still tempted to think the same today.

1984 Ferrari 288 GTO

Of the many cars that could have made it into my personal Top Ten of the best supercars of all time, it is perhaps the Ferrari 288GTO from 1984 that has the strongest case. Fans of the GTO consider it to be the most important supercar of all time, possibly the first ever hypercar, and therefore they would probably replace the Ferrari F40 in my Top Ten with this Ferrari masterpiece. Why?

First up, the back story. The car was launched at the Geneva Motor Show in 1984. Taking the 1977 Ferrari 308GTB Speciale as a design cue, the idea was to create a car that could be raced in the Group B GT formula. However, by the time Ferrari were knee-deep in creating this special car, that particular race series had collapsed due to a lack of manufacturer interest. So, the 288GTO's entire *raison d'être* was suddenly obsolete, and consequently the car never raced.

In a sense, though, this faltering start made the car all the more desirable, not least because owners liked knowing it had been designed to be a race monster. A quick look at the specifications sheet confirms that Ferrari had indeed created a rare beast. And, although there is a lineage from the 308GTB, the 288GTO was radically different in many ways: twin turbos were added – the very first use of such turbos in a Ferrari road car – and the engine was a 2855cc, all-alloy V8, longitudinally placed with the gearbox in line, meaning the car had no rear boot at all. Ferrari also added electronic injection and ignition systems, based on their contemporary F1 set up.

ABOVE ***Less well-known than its headline-grabbing successor, the F40, the 288GTO is actually considered the more important car by many purists.***

What really startled many observers, though, was that Ferrari had chosen to cloak this car in a revolutionary body. At the time, lightweight components such as Kevlar and carbon were limited to race cars, but the 288GTO was lavished with these expensive and high-tech materials, with the construction overseen by British engineer Dr Harvey Postlethwaite. Components such as Kevlar in the tail and rear bulkhead, moulded fibreglass and carbon fibre in the roof, and aluminium honeycomb in the firewall made this the first Ferrari to boast this kind of composite construction. These high-tech body panels made the car an extraordinary 250lb lighter than the already lightweight 308GTB. This was truly ground-breaking.

In addition, the car's power seemed visibly to be straining to get out of the bodywork – the Pininfarina-designed silhouette used flared wheel arches, housing massive tyres, as well as generous and stylish side scoops in the doors

ABOVE ***The quadruple driving lights and front spoiler are distinctive 288GTO features.***

and rear quarters, plus a front spoiler that made the car hug the ground. Two design elements that were directly influenced by the famous 250GTO were the rear spoiler and the air slats behind the rear wheels, which were very similar to the ones found behind the front wheels of the 1960s racer. Periscope-like side mirrors were in the classic 1980s style, while the slats on the rear deck lid (used for cooling the turbo) added further visual drama.

Impressively, this huge power and performance was matched by a stylish interior of (very 1980s) red-and-black leather seats. Optional extras were pricey, and even at the base price of £60,000 ($100,000) you didn't get a radio cassette player. The instruments were criticised by some as looking cheap, although the turbo boost gauge was always going to excite. The 288GTO had the potential to lull the inexperienced into a false sense of security: at low revs the car seemed to behave well, but when the turbo gauge hit 3,000rpm, the noise was said to resemble 'a blood-curdling howl' – at which point the handling could best be described as 'feisty'.

The 288GTO was the fastest road-going Ferrari in production on its launch, with a 0–60mph time of 4.9 seconds and a top speed of 189mph. Yet, as the almost universally positive reviews confirmed, it was still very easy to drive, even around town at low speeds.

Ferrari were so proud of their work that they gave the car the GTO moniker – at the time only one other vehicle owned that name, the legendary

ABOVE ***The 288GTO would open the door to the fabled Ferrari F40 and is now regarded as one of the most prized and collectible of all the 1980s supercars.***

250GTO (and only one has earned it since, the 599GTO of 2010). In the end, the planned figure of 200 cars needed for homologation (that is, to qualify the car for racing) was upped to 272, all of which sold almost instantly. When five Evoluzione models were made – which were more powerful and more aggressively styled – this already heated market became even more excitable. In fact, stories started to emerge of people paying huge premiums above the list price to get hold of a car, which has led some to credit the 288GTO with the invention of the modern supercar 'investors' market.

So, to answer the question I posed at the start of this entry, the main reason the 288GTO is a candidate to replace the F40, in my personal Top Ten, is because its use of composite materials and numerous other technologies was a first on the supercar scene. Simply put, without the 288GTO there would be no F40. And all this is to miss one, final, vitally important point: the 288GTO is absolutely beautiful. Some supercars are flamboyant, some are aggressive, some are sleek, but has there ever been a more *beautiful* example of the genre?

1984 Ferrari Testarossa

If the brutal 288GTO has come to be hailed by purists as one of the greatest Ferrari's ever made, the arguably more famous – in non-petrol-head circles at least – Testarossa of 1984 has always polarised opinion far more. This was a flat-12 Ferrari designed to be much more refined than the racy 288GTO, more luxurious and also more commercial. Taking its name from the legendary racing Ferraris that enjoyed so much success in the late 1950s and early 1960s, the Testarossa's name meant 'red head' – a reference to the red-painted valve covers.

The car was launched in Paris, in 1984, to mixed reviews. Many critics disliked the visual signature that would actually become the car's trademark look – the distinctive slats running down the sides of the doors and body. Known as 'strakes', these long grills were functional – they cooled the radiators that Ferrari had moved from the front of the car to in front of the rear wheels. The strakes continued a theme found in the rear lights, which were hidden behind a mean-looking grill, while the skeletal side mirrors set a new style that would be mimicked by dozens of rival supercars.

Another criticism levelled at it was of the massive width of the car – again a trademark feature – that made the Testarossa half an inch wider than a Range Rover. It was a very long car, too – a foot longer than its main rival, the Lamborghini Countach.

The Testarossa needed a lot of air to cool its pretty sizeable power plant, which was an evolution of the 512BB block that used a mid-engined, 4.9-litre, flat-12 producing 390bhp. This made it the fastest car in the world on its launch, with a top speed of 180mph. The gearbox sat above the engine, meaning the centre of gravity was higher, which at times made high-speed handling rather iffy.

BELOW ***The striking Testarossa was slightly wider than a Range Rover. Like anyone cares. Which one would you buy?***

The Testarossa also had aluminium panels, a tubular steel frame and big brakes. The rearward placement of the radiators meant the cabin was cooler, too, fixing a problem that had plagued its predecessor, the 512BB. The layout also offered more luggage space and a larger interior. Ferrari said this cabin was 'a living room at 180mph', with air-conditioning as standard, a very 1980s central console and stitched leather seats. Luxury was very much the philosophy of the car, quite in contrast to the stripped-back F40. The soft, comfortable ride also had decent visibility all round. And, as a bonus, there was also a vanity mirror that popped up when you opened the glove box!

With such a very refined drive, the car was already hugely appealing to a wider customer market before the Testarossa appeared for several series in the hugely popular US cop show *Miami Vice*, as Sonny Crockett's car. This further helped to send sales soaring to their final figure of 7,200 units, making it the brand's best-ever seller.

The car did undergo some evolution in its lifetime. The 512 TR was a radical departure, with a more rounded nose, a heavily revamped engine offering greater power, better fuel economy, a lighter, stiffer, upgraded chassis, and improved overall performance. The swansong was to be a 512M, with even greater power and new lights. Added to that, these later editions had cleaner emissions, which helped US sales.

Ultimately, although not universally popular, the Ferrari Testarossa is a definitive, 1980s poster supercar.

ABOVE ***Either a staged, picturesque photo or the world's first-ever, cross-country Ferrari. You decide!***

OVERLEAF ***The Testarossa's distinctive side strakes. Critics have dubbed the side vents 'egg slicers' or 'cheese graters'.***

GAME CHANGER

1985 Porsche 959

ABOVE ***The most technologically advanced car of its day: the Porsche 959.***

THE SECOND HALF OF THE 1980S WITNESSED a heavyweight battle of supercars that would have made any boxing promoter proud, as the technical masterpiece that was the Porsche 959 faced off against the brutally sparse racing monster – the Ferrari F40. First into the ring was the 959...

Launched in 1985, the Porsche 959 was the most technologically advanced supercar ever seen. It was also the fastest, one of the most expensive, and certainly one of the most elite cars of all time. Part of the reason for this was that the Porsche 959 was a child of one of motorsport's most lunatic eras: Group B.

Covering road as well as rally racing, Group B regulations stated that manufacturers had to build a minimum of 200 machines for road use in order to qualify but in return there was *no limit* set on the brake horsepower. Consequently, marques such as Lancia, Ford, Jaguar, Peugeot and Audi went completely nuts, creating the motorsport equivalents of Frankenstein's monster. So fast and brutal were these Group B behemoths that some would have been capable of qualifying as high as sixth on the Formula 1 grid of the day.

Stepping back in time a little further, though, unearths the first seeds of this magical new Porsche. By the end of the 1970s, there were murmurings that perhaps the 911 was in its Indian summer, that the rear-engined supercar was a relic, and that the vogue for mid-engine poise would ultimately snuff out this particular Germanic icon. However, Porsche were not so pessimistic, and the initial idea for the 959 was an exercise in seeing how far the 911 could be evolved.

BELOW ***The brilliant-white Gruppe B car, essentially a prototype of the 959, complete with striking, flat alloys.***

In 1981, an all-wheel-drive, one-off 911 was shown at the Frankfurt Motor Show. Two years later, a similar model, modified for rallying, won the Paris-Dakar Rally, complete with pioneering torque vectoring technology and four-wheel drive. Then, in 1983, Porsche stunned the world with a fabulous concept car, known as 'Gruppe B' – in theory, designed for racing in that brutal class. This new car was in brilliant white, with deeper inset lights and modernistic, flat alloys. In fact, this was the first hint of the 959 to come and contained many elements of the eventual production car.

However, for all its brilliance, the 959 suffered a slow gestation. The technical demands of the project were inevitably very challenging and problems with American legislation provided another stumbling block. In 1985, the 959 was officially unveiled to the public at the Frankfurt Motor Show, but actual deliveries would not start until early 1987. By then, Group B rallying had been abandoned, but the thirst for this revolutionary, new left-hand-drive Porsche supercar was unabated, even at an eye-watering price of £140,000 ($236,000) – five times that of a standard 911 of the day.

The six-speed manual gearbox, with computer-controlled four-wheel drive, propelled the 959 to 60mph in just 3.7 seconds, 100mph in 8.3 seconds, and then on to a top speed of 197mph. All this established the 959 as the fastest street-legal car in the world on its launch.

Alex Karidis is one of the UK's most prominent plastic surgeons. His job involves 'perfecting' people's bodies and faces, refining what they have been given by nature, and he is clearly exceptionally good at it. This pre-eminence has allowed him to indulge his passion for supercars and rare classics. I met Alex in northwest London when he picked me up in his commuter car, a dashing 911 GT3. He was immaculately dressed and quietly well-spoken, accommodating and friendly. We spoke about supercars and it was immediately apparent that Alex has a great knowledge of the genre, much of which gained through owning various specimens himself. We drove to a secret lock-up under the bowels of an apartment block, squeezed down an impossibly narrow entrance and parked up next to a white, locked door. Alex opened the door and I walked into a small room, to be met by three brutish examples of Peugeot's Group B rally cars. Ordinarily these historic beasts would have kept my attention for some time, but I wasn't here for them – I was here for the gleaming 959 in the corner.

After admiring the 959 for some time, I asked Alex why he bought this mid-1980s supercar. 'Everyone was aware of the 959. Along with the F40, it is one of the posters on your wall, right? I was aware of Group B, too. I had lived through that but I never had a 959 directly on my radar. At the time, they were hugely expensive and I was not in a position to buy one. But I always looked through the adverts, anyway! Then, one day, I went on to a car website, like we all do, and BANG! This car was for sale. It was low in mileage, had a special colour (most were either silver, red or black, and this is a special-order 'media grey'), and it was the only one in the UK. I put a deposit down by wire transfer there and then. Hey, it's a 959, what is there not to like?!'

That unusual paintwork was still in showroom condition when I came to visit, and Alex told me the car had only done 8,000 miles. This was a car brimming with state-of-the-art tech when it was launched. Perhaps the most headline-grabbing element was the all-wheel drive system – although the Audi Quattro was already using four-wheel drive, many consider the 959 to be the first true supercar to make use of that technology. The drive system offered four settings: dry, wet, snow, and off-road. The car's power was controlled, depending on these settings and the actual driving demands at the time, so that the car would constantly shift power between the front and rear wheels. The fancy word for this is 'torque vectoring', which sounds about as space-age as the system was at the time. As Alex rightly says, 'This was a technical tour de force when it came out'.

The technological parade didn't stop there. The computer-controlled brakes had ABS, the steering had servo-assist (what we now know as power steering), and both the ride height and suspension stiffness were variable. Tyre pressure monitors and run-flat tyres were also included (negating the need for spare tyres), staple items on many cars in the modern era, but revolutionary at the time.

The more conventional aspects of the car were by no means modest, either. The engine was a 2850cc, flat-6 – rear-mounted as in the 911 – that generated 450bhp at 6,500rpm. To add to the sophistication, the engine was fitted with twin KKK turbos that were sequential – meaning that rather than two turbos kicking in at the same time and trying to send the 959 into space, they did so in sequence. The idea was to make the boost more progressive, rather than producing the neck-break, guttural punch of cars such as the F40. This was refinement, not savagery. Visually, the turbo plumes are very dramatic. While Porsche engines are usually covered up, in a typically understated fashion, the 959 shows off more than most.

LEFT *The Porsche 959's engine is a little more overtly sinuous and powerful than the usually more sedate 911 power plant.*

In later years, purist Porsche fanatics would be horrified by a switch from air- to water-cooling for the 911, but – technically speaking – the 959 actually uses both methods. Alex again: 'They say the 996 is the first water-cooled Porsche, but in fact *this* is the first water-cooled one, because it has water-cooled heads. It has an air-cooled engine block, yes, but water-cooled heads.' The car has a petrol cap in the bonnet, as well as one behind both doors, for the oil and fluids.

And what did all this high-tech look like? In 1985, Ferry Porsche said, 'It has always been our philosophy that function and beauty are inseparable.' Maybe so, but the 959 has had its critics in terms of style. The very long tail created a tiny drag coefficient, which Porsche claimed ensured zero lift, but style connoisseurs were not universally impressed. Actually, only the tail light was from a 911, while the rest of the bodywork was unique to the 959. In the flesh, the tail does indeed look long, but the car is also

ABOVE ***The Porsche 959 squared up to a Ferrari F40 in a supercar Battle Royale.***

BB PW 916

far more muscular, and at the same time more curvaceous, than photos in magazines would suggest. The scoops on the doors are aggressive and eye-catching in real life. The rear arches are huge, in fact ten inches wider than the contemporary 911 Turbo, itself a very wide car. The 959 also had a flatter, sharper nose. Sure, it is no F40, but nor is this an ugly duckling.

'In terms of aesthetics,' continues Alex, 'I will be honest: it is not the most beautiful car. However, it doesn't need to be. I think there is too much overhang on that long tail, but for Porsche it was all about function. The longer tail helped the aerodynamics and downforce. Form and function for me are key; they are interlinked. And I am someone who works with their hands, so I appreciate craftsmanship, workmanship and engineering. I may not understand it like an engineer but I appreciate it.'

This opinion-dividing bodywork sat on a steel monocoque and used an aluminium bonnet and doors mixed with Kevlar panels – for extreme lightness. In addition, the plastic panels were 50 per cent lighter than their steel equivalent. Some owners reported rippling in the doors, caused by the mirrors being heavy and the doors so light. Although any supercar worth its salt, produced post-2000, would be dripping with Kevlar and/or carbon fibre, at the time of the 959's creation the use of such lightweight materials was innovative. This edict for lightness was extended to the featherweight, magnesium alloy wheels. 'Most of my cars are pre-1990, mid- or rear-engine and all plastic-bodied – I am a plastic surgeon after all! I like lightweight, it is the way to go. Even so, the build quality of the 959 is amazing. When you slam the doors shut it sounds superb. Porsche engineering, see?'

The interior disappointed some owners, as Alex explains: 'The seats were standard 911, as were most of the dials and the switch gear. The 959 logo on the steering wheel was one of the few differences. The windscreen was more angled and bonded than with the 911, and it is very expensive to replace! But some owners felt short-changed after spending so much money and getting, essentially, a 911 interior. Mine has the original cassette player, and I even have the cassette that came with it, which has this audio saying something like, 'Thank you for purchasing this Porsche. You are now sitting in the most sophisticated vehicle the world has ever known!'

The car had a limited production run: though precise numbers are hard to pin down, it is in the region of 283 units (there were some prototypes and later, USA-modified models, too). Despite the huge interest in the car – with some reports suggesting customers were offering as much as $1 million to get one – the rumour was that Porsche were losing between $150,000 and $300,000 on each sale. However, the 959 – like the Veyron of nearly 20 years later – was a technical exercise as well as a global showcase for what the company could do. In that sense, the 959 was a resounding success.

Porsche has a long heritage of motorsport success but, ironically, the 959 – their most advanced car to date – was decidedly muted in this field. It achieved an impressive 1–2 at the 1986 Paris-Dakar Rally and came seventh in Le Mans (first in its class), but that was pretty much that. Due to the Group B class being abandoned after some tragic fatalities, the 959 never raced in this category at all.

LEFT ***The famous all-wheel drive system was controlled by the Porsche Steuer Kupplung (also known as the PSK) gear box with four settings, all computer controlled. The gearbox consisted of 13 wheels in an oil bath – an extremely complex system then and now. First gear was called the 'G-gear' – gelande – or 'cross-county'.***

ABOVE *The Dakar Rally 959.*

Prior to the 959, the majority of supercars capable of such heady speeds were heavy and hard to drive, but the 959 was easy. At very high speeds the engine was almost quiet, with minimal cabin noise. Some criticised this aspect of the car, saying it was so technologically advanced that it had erased human involvement. This, they suggested, was excellence but not exuberance.

Given everything, can the 959 be considered the best Porsche ever? Alex is clear on this question: 'The best-built Porsche, yes, and the best technology. All this stuff filtered through – the four-wheel drive system, the suspension – all these things ended up in later generations, so this has to be seen as the mother of modern Porsches. Whether it is as exciting to drive as a '73 RS… probably not. The RS is a very light and fast car, but the 959 is a different type of machine. If you want a better car, then there is no question that this is is the more complete all-rounder.

'The 959 drives fantastically well, much smoother than my 964, in fact. You drop the clutch and, boom!, it is gone. It holds itself up very nicely to modern Porsches. Ride comfort is great, the suspension is brilliant, those dual shocks and springs and double wishbones all round make it much more supple. It's very easy to drive, not stiff at all. That it is so subtle and easy to drive explains why some 959s have 60–70,000 miles on the clock. If I had to take one car to go across Europe, the 959 would be it, no question.

SUPERCAR FACT

959 Sport: There was a more extreme Sport version built (the standard model was called Confort – correct spelling with the 'n'). There were possibly as few as six but possibly as many as 29 of these Sport models made; each of which was 100kg lighter than the standard model, with no air-conditioning, electric windows or even right-hand wing mirror. The engine generated an extra 64bhp.

RIGHT *US regulations stopped the 959 from being imported, initially, but in 2001 a change in the law allowed a limited number of cars to filter into the USA. One US company cleverly modified numerous examples, boosting power to over 600bhp. This resulted in a sensational 0–60mph time of 3.2 seconds and a top speed of 215mph.*

'I regularly get dealers 'phoning me up to ask if I would like to sell it. For me, it is an undervalued car. It is only now approaching the cost of when it was launched, in real terms, while other cars have far greater values even though they are dogs to drive. But you don't buy a 959 for that, you buy it for passion. This is a keeper.'

The 959's use of state-of-the-art technology, such as four-wheel drive, makes it a game changer. In many ways, this car raised the game in terms of the high-tech requirements for a world-leading supercar. The 959 also set a precedent for all future Porsches, as a crowning example of the filter-down benefits of supercars to their mass-production cousins.

Alex often uses his 959, not least because he believes such cars need to be fired up frequently. 'You do have to drive it regularly, because they can seize up. So, every three or four weeks, I take it out for a spin. They need to be driven. The technology was pioneering back then, but now it tends to seize up if you don't use it.

'I buy cars to drive. When I drive my 959 I know I am driving history. I know what impact this car had, and that is an important part of classic car ownership. Every important classic car has its place in history, and this is one of the most significant cars in automotive history.' Standing there, looking at the 959 – which is surprisingly striking as it crouchs down powerfully in that corner of a secret London garage – it's hard to disagree with him.

Porsche 959

LAUNCHED

1985

POWER

450bhp

ACCELERATION

0–60mph in 3.9 secs

MAXIMUM SPEED

196mph

PRODUCTION RUN

292 units

GAME CHANGER

1987 Ferrari F40

ABOVE ***The F40 is the definitive 1980s supercar and arguably the best Ferrari ever.***

ASK MOST TEN-YEAR-OLDS TO DRAW A SUPERCAR on a blank piece of paper, and the majority would probably sketch a red, wedge-shaped machine with a big wing on its back end. Or, to put it another way, they would draw a Ferrari F40. Just to be clear, I am not likening the legendary design skills of Pininfarini to the drawing ability of a ten-year-old. In fact, I am paying the F40 the highest compliment. It means that, in a sense, the F40 represents the supercar of the subconscious, the dream car of the senses, and therefore – by definition – arguably the greatest supercar silhouette of them all.

The F40 was a game changer, of that there is no question. Prior to the F40, most supercars were huge in size and had normally aspirated engines – often V12s – so the V8, twin-turbo F40 was a watershed moment in supercar history.

In the summer of 1986, Enzo Ferrari had asked his team to create a new car to celebrate the fortieth anniversary of the brand the following year. The much-anticipated car had been dubbed the 'Le Mans' Ferrari and was to be the successor to the mighty 288GTO. The car was also Ferrari's response to the high-tech Porsche 959. Ferrari was unashamed that this new F40 was a road car, born on the track, and using technology drawn from their race teams. Looking at it, the car is clearly influenced by Ferraris from the 1960s, too, with its very Italian, sleek, and angular looks.

Fast-forward a year to July 1987, at Maranello's museum, and an 89-year-old Enzo Ferrari himself was on hand to launch the car that many now consider to be his brand's crowning achievement. The invite to the press pack said simply, 'If you happen to be in Modena this particular day, you might be interested in seeing this new car.'

BELOW ***The F40's front bonnet and rear boot raised up.***

RIGHT ***The F40's aggressive scoops and air-intakes are classic supercar details.***

For my part, I was hugely interested to see this car as I headed over to the Essex home of Liam Howlett, of electronic band The Prodigy. Three previous hook-ups with Liam had been arranged, only to be cancelled owing to his band's increasing and unavoidable commitments. I didn't mind one iota, because I knew this fabled supercar, about which I had heard so much, was waiting at the end of this particular sub-bass rainbow.

Finally, the day arrived and I headed to Essex on the train once more. Arriving at Liam's house, the massive double gates slid open silently and he came out to meet me. The kettle was boiled, chat was had, and then Liam said, 'So, do you wanna see the F40 then, man?'

I did. I *really, really* did.

We walked across his lawn and towards a number of pristine-looking garages. As we approached, Liam took a remote fob out of his pocket and pressed it. I stood there, noticing my raised heart-rate, and watched as the door started to open. When it was about six inches off the ground I saw the prancing horse badge and then, a few seconds later, the whole car was revealed.

It is hard to describe seeing an F40 in the metal for the first time. It is quite simply breathtaking. Jaw-dropping. All of that and then some. It is *so aggressive*. The slanted nose hugs the tarmac and the NACA ducts in the bonnet hint at the power at the driver's disposal. This thing clearly needs oxygen. *Lots* of oxygen. The side architecture is just incredible – those two big scoops dug out of the door and rear side panel, and the eye-catching outer sill. The rear of the car is simply a work of art. The Plexiglass engine cover – yes, plastic, we will come to that in a moment – and more ducts. Then, of course, that iconic rear wing with the F40 name embossed in its vertical struts. The car is larger in life than you expect, but all the more fabulous for that. The F40 was only available in Rossa Corsa (racing red). In fact, all Ferraris built between 1987 and 1992 were red with red interior detailing. It was also built only in left-hand-drive, with the exception of seven cars commissioned for the Middle East.

Liam could see my reaction and he was just smiling, he didn't need to say anything. I opened the passenger door and climbed in to what can only be described as a pure race car. I pulled the door shut using a piece of cable (there's no handle) and sat in one of the bucket seats, with its three-point harness. Beyond that, there is a basic carpeting inside and pretty much nothing else. Each owner could choose from just three seat types and would visit the factory for a personal fitting. The seats were plastic composite and weighed just 3lb each. Air-conditioning was available, because the cabin got so hot, but electric windows were not an option. Instead, only sliding windows were initially on offer (manual, wind-up windows were later made). The interior of Liam's car is all in black felt except for the seats and door panels. Old-school gauges, rather than the forthcoming vogue of LED instrument panels, pepper the minimal dash. There was no ABS, no power steering, no brake servo, no airbags, no central locking, and a radio only as an optional extra. You wouldn't really be able to hear it over the screaming engine, though, anyway.

The frugality of the inside was matched externally. *Anything* that didn't add performance was not tolerated. The bodywork was a combination of 11 panels of carbon fibre, Kevlar and aluminium – highly innovative for a road car at the time. The joints were glued, to save weight, and the green adhesive was left clearly visible. The front bonnet only weighed 40lb. Each door, fully kitted, was just 3.3lb. The iconic rear wing was a necessity to create downforce and was chiselled in a wind tunnel by the Pininfarina design team – led by Leonardo Fioravanti, who had also designed the Daytona, the 512BB, the 308GTB and the Boxer Ferraris. The front windscreen was glass, and the other windows were plastic. The car had two fuel cells, one either side of the rear wheels. The cells were constructed from a very lightweight material, so they would need to be replaced every ten years.

In order to keep the weight down further, only two litres of Ferrari red paint were used. The thin covering was so slight that you could see the composite weave under the red paint. For this reason, lots of F40s have subsequently been resprayed.

BELOW ***Earlier, pre-catalytic converter models are more valuable, and several have nudged 500bhp when tested, supporting the theory that most F40s delivered more bhp than the manufacturer suggested. High-profile owners have included Nigel Mansell, Alain Prost, Nick Mason, Jay Kay and Chris Evans.***

The engine was a relatively 'modest' 2.9-litre V8, evolved from the power plant found in the twin-turbo 288GTO, but with the addition of two larger turbo chargers and two intercoolers, which catapulted the F40's output to 478bhp at 7,000rpm – with a frankly ludicrous 426lb/foot of torque at just 4,000rpm. The car came with a five-speed manual gearbox, available with or without a synchro-mesh.

Those scoops and ducts, now so iconic, were not simply for show: the NACA ducts cool the interior while the two others on the sides cool the brakes and engine bay. Further hot air is released via the duct behind each front wheel arch. The plastic engine cover might look low-tech, but it was actually shaped precisely to direct air flow over that famous large rear wing. When all of this aerodynamic design was wrapped around a car weighing just 1,104kg, the performance was prodigious.

This attention to weight-saving was matched by the car's brutal power output. Therefore, the F40 had predictably apocalyptic performance consequences. Its 0–60mph was just 3.8 seconds, but it was the top speed that grabbed all the headlines: the F40 was the first road car to exceed 200mph – 201mph to be precise. The speedometer actually went up to 225mph, and a tuned F40 is reported to have reached 226mph on the Bonneville salt flats. The car was, therefore – by definition – the fastest in the world when it was launched, and it cost nearly £200,000 ($340,000).

RIGHT ***The F40 pretty much ticks every box in terms of supercar silhouettes, with features such as scoops, intakes, and rear spoilers, as well as sheer road presence.***

Innovative injection and ignition-management technology, taken from the Ferrari F1 team, made starting up the F40 easy and predictable. However, after that point you are really in the hands of the gods. When driven hard, the car makes all manner of weird and wonderful clanks and whizzes.

Ferrari could only build one, sometimes two F40s a day, and as such production was initially limited to around 300 cars. However, the demand was so great that they eventually made 1,315 cars – making it Ferrari's most profitable car up to that point. Some owners criticised this higher-than-expected number for diluting their investment. That said, it was perhaps one of the very first examples of a supercar being made in a specified, limited number. There was an even more extreme version, the F40 LM, converted by Michelotto in Padova – with a frankly ludicrous power boost to 700bhp – which was itself capable of being tuned to 900bhp for race days. Ironically, the F40 didn't achieve the rash of race wins you might have expected, but, let's face it, no one really cares about that.

I asked Liam why he had been drawn to buy the F40. 'I first heard about the F40 in the late 1980s, mainly because it was the first 200mph supercar, and also I knew about the crazy prices some people paid for them. I was never a Ferrari fan as a teen. I always felt the '80s road Ferraris were a bit 'Rod Stewart', apart from the 288GTO, which is beautiful and where the idea of the F40 started. My first trip in an F40 was through a friend whose dad had one. I remember being terrified, sitting in the passenger seat, belting down a country lane. I don't like being driven fast as a passenger.

'By the mid-1990s I had bought a Diablo SV and wasn't happy with the quality. It was in the pre-Audi days. I think I'd had that car a month when

I heard there were two F40s for sale at a local dealer. So, I did the deal and traded in the Diablo, which was slow and lumbering compared to the F40. I did lots of homework before driving it and ended up going for the 'pre-cat' car, which apparently had more power than the later cars. My car was one of the first 50, identified by the sliding Lexan windows. I remember it was the cheaper of the two cars for sale and wasn't in perfect showroom condition, but that was fine; I just drove it hard and didn't ever worry about preserving it.

'One thing for sure is that the F40 is not a car you can just jump in and drive, regardless of whichever car you have driven before. You have to respect it at all times and always be aware of road surface moisture. I remember when I first sat in the car, I loved the fact you could see the joins in the footwells, the basic, felt-covered dashboard – who uses felt? – and the drilled pedals. It all added to the road racer appeal. The only leather used was on the steering wheel.

'It is possible to drive it like a 'normal' car below 3,500 revs, but after that point the turbos light up and you have to be aware of that when cornering. When the turbo boosts it is an instant wall of power that can catch you out and put the car quickly out of shape. That shocked me the first time I drove it. I wasn't expecting the rear wheels to spin at 100mph. And my car was fitted with a Michelotto exhaust system, so there was minimal turbo noise by way of warning. At high speed it is very settled for a car of that age; it pulls away real hard, still over 140, and just keeps going. The only area I think could have been improved is the brakes. A couple of owners I spoke to have had them upgraded.

'With any car I've owned, just being fast is never enough. Handling goes without saying but it's got to have drama, too – it has to make you feel excited just sitting in it. The F40 has that. I always loved the Porsche 2.7 Carrera RS – stripped-out, no luxuries, purposeful. That's exactly what the F40 is like. It is an out-and-out, pure, raw, driver's car. The way the car feels on the road is the reason it's number one for me. The steering gives you direct, precise feedback at all times – no power assist and none needed. You always feel totally connected to it, unlike the Enzo where I felt like there was a computer between me and the car. The Enzo is easy to drive compared to the F40, but it just doesn't have that same raw drama.

'My fondest memory of my F40 was when The Prodigy had a press day in England with the Japanese media. It was roughly a half-hour drive so I thought I'd take the F40. I went round to pick [Prodigy band-mate, the 'Firestarter'] Keef up and when I got there he had a 7-foot albino python around his neck. Keef said was it cool to bring it and not to worry because this snake had eaten a few hours before. We jumped in and set off – this was the first time Keef had been in the car and he was fully shocked when I floored it – just a load of swear words came out. The snake had slid into the passenger door hollow by then and was chilling in there. We pulled into the hotel where the Japanese press team were standing outside, waiting, but we had forgotten about the snake by this time. Keef got out and a couple of the Japanese guys came over to greet us but also wanted to look at the car. So, this one journalist opened the passenger door and nearly had a heart attack

Ferrari F40

LAUNCHED

1987

POWER

478bhp

ACCELERATION

0–60mph in 3.8 secs

MAXIMUM SPEED

A tuned F40 is reported to have reached 226mph on the Bonneville salt flats.

PRODUCTION RUN

Production was initially limited to around 300 cars. However, demand was so great that Ferrari eventually made 1,315 cars.

seeing this massive white-and-yellow snake curled up in the door. He was really freaking out in front of 20 other Japanese journos. Keef calmly walked up, pulled the python out, put it round his neck and walked into the hotel. It was a good way to start off the interviews.

'Talking now about what the F40 delivered, in this time of a new wave of supercars, almost makes certain aspects of it seem normal. The new supercars have the speed, acceleration and handling, but gone are the days of raw, drivers' cars like the F40. I sold my F40, after a few years, to a fella who wrapped it around a tree two weeks later, destroying it. I don't know why I sold it and I wish I hadn't.'

The F40 is arguably the greatest-ever Ferrari and that, combined with its 200mph top speed and raw, even savage, approach to driving makes it a game changer. The launch of the F40, back in July 1987, was Enzo Ferrari's last public appearance, and in 1988 he passed away. This savage, brutal, brilliant masterpiece was his worthy swansong.

BELOW **Enzo Ferrari's greatest ever creation?**

Also in the 1980s

1980 Caterham Seven Based on the 1968 version of the 1957 Lotus Seven, using a Ford engine, the Seven started a range of cars that offer you the most fun you can have on a track without being a professional driver.

1980 Matra Murena Following on from the notoriously rusty Bagheera, this under-rated, modestly priced French supercar had a galvanised chassis and fibreglass bodywork.

1981 Lamborghini Jalpa Intended as a more affordable Lamborghini than the Countach, the Jalpa had a 3.5-litre V8 engine, rather than the usual V12, but it still sold fairly well.

1984 Ferrari Mondial Pininfarina-styled and wedge-shaped.

LEFT ***The Ferrari Mondial.***

BELOW ***The Lamborghini Jalpa.***

ABOVE **The Aston Martin Vantage Zagato V8.**

ABOVE RIGHT **The Renault Alpine GTA Turbo.**

1984 Marcos Mantula Marcos Mantula was a 1960s marque that was revitalised in the 1980s with a strong Rover V8 engine. The car has a unique silhouette.

1986 Aston Martin V8 Vantage Aston Martin found themselves trailing behind somewhat during the 1970s, with several potentially great cars struggling from a lack of development. Picking up on the rich heritage of the Zagato DB4GT, the four-seater Vantage was limited to just 50 coupes and 25 convertibles, all of which were brutally fast but very expensive. The brutish 5.4-litre V8 provided single-figure miles-per-gallon under hard driving, making a full tank's range around 250 miles. The straight-line speed was ballistic, faster than a contemporary 911 Turbo. It went to 200mph, which led some to label it as Britain's first, genuine homegrown supercar. Each engine was hand built by one of four Aston specialists – one man did the entire job, in each case leaving a small brass plaque, bearing his name,

on the engine block. This came at a price – the car cost ten per cent more than the great Ferrari Boxer, but nonetheless the Vantage successfully blew away the cobwebs of Aston Martin's 1970s, middle-aged spread.

1986 Renault Alpine GTA Alpine were rally masters and renowned for their genius with fibreglass, rear-engine layouts and the cutting-edge use of polyester components. For this classic French supercar, they teamed up with Renault, using a 2.8-litre V6 that was surprisingly powerful. The lightweight construction allowed for very nimble handling, while the turbo version was mad. At the time of writing this book, there is rumoured to be a new Renault Alpine being readied for both road and racing.

1989 Ferrari 348 The 348 had side strakes reminiscent of the Testatrossa, but it was distinctly unpleasant to drive. The car enjoyed some race success. But...Hummm. Try driving one.

What about?

Here is a selection of really significant cars that are worthy of further investigation. They might not be game changers, or even the most high-profile cars of their era, but the following vehicles deserve special mention.

1984 TVR 350i
1989 Panther Solo

The 1990s

LEFT ***The Diablo was a more understated Lambo than the Countach, but still a frankly bonkers supercar.***

The 1990s began with a severe recession that brought an abrupt end to the 1980s consumer (and supercar) boom. Sales of luxury brands, including supercars, were hammered and several marques succumbed to the economic downturn. Eventually, the financial gloom would lift, but it was a long period of austerity for manufacturers to endure. That said, this decade that saw the rise of mobile phones and the internet also welcomed several new members to the 200mph-plus club, such as the Jaguar XJ220, the Bugatti EB110, the Lamborghini Diablo and the Ferrari F50. All was not lost in the supercar world.

During the 1960s, Le Mans cars were often tweaked and made useable for the road. However, by the 1990s, those racers were beyond everyday road use and so, in their place, GT cars began to filter through into road-going versions. In terms of 1990s supercar history, there was one car that completely and utterly overshadowed everything else on the planet, from its launch in 1992 until well into the 2000s. That car was the astonishing McLaren F1. This car would set a benchmark that would remain unchallenged for well over a decade. To this day, the F1 is considered by many to be the greatest supercar of them all. As we shall see...

ABOVE ***The Lamborghini Diablo continued the marque's tradition of making super-fast, ultra-striking supercars.***

ABOVE **The Lamborghini Diablo 6.0 litre.**

1990 Lamborghini Diablo

The Diablo became the fastest production car in the world on its launch in January 1990, with the dawn of the new decade. Finding a worthy successor to the Countach was always going to be a tricky task, but the Diablo – meaning 'Devil' – also had to cope with the challenge of much tougher emissions and safety legislation. In true Lamborghini style, they stuck with a massive aluminium V12 – this time a 5.7-litre producing 492bhp. That decision represented two fingers to the new noise and emissions rules. And this power created performance that obliterated the Countach: 0–60mph in 3.6 seconds – for the quickest Diablo – and with a top speed of 210mph on some models. Lamborghini developed the all-alloy block from the Countach and tuned it to new extremes.

The Diablo's bodywork was a mixture of lightweight materials – alloy, steel and composite – sitting over a fairly traditional steel space-frame. Mostly handmade – including the engine and many body panels – although, with some help from robots, there was still the sense this car had been made by Italian artisans. The shell was generously filled with scoops and ducts to aid with air flow and cooling, all of which added to the drama. And there was yet more drama every time the Diablo drove over a speed bump or down a parking ramp, because its ground clearance was so slight! The car was also very long, very heavy and very wide.

The Miura and Countach designer, Gandini, was brought on board for 'Project 132'. He created a longer shape for the Diablo than its famous predecessor with fewer frills, but still with a muscular look. (New owners Chrysler were reported to have altered Gandini's original shape somewhat.) The Diablo seemed to become more unruly as it aged, with a four-wheel-drive version (although notably only 27% of drive went to the front) offering stunning traction. This was followed by lighter, more powerful monsters such as the outrageous SE30 and white-knuckle SV. More fins and scoops were added to these later examples, as well as a greater use of carbon fibre. The VT Roadster was equally sensational. Over its 11-year life span, there were as many as 15 Diablo variations, with the last versions built by new owner, Audi.

Entrance to the Diablo was via fabulous scissor doors. And from inside, the nose dropped away so quickly that the driver wouldn't be able to see the road from their seat, only instruments then tarmac. The interior was merely adequate. A 'crunchy' gearbox and some reliability and build issues were also reported.

As a result, the Diablo was no Miura or Countach, and initially it was also overshadowed by the watershed Porsche 959 and Ferrari F40. For that reason, perhaps the Diablo has received less praise than it might deserve. After all, it sold 2,884 examples, so it was at least commercially successful and one must remember that the slowest Diablo could notch up a highly impressive 202mph. Despite its flaws, this was still a loud, visually striking, and raucous Lamborghini, with looks, performance and presence to boot. In a sense, by retaining so many of the old-school qualities of a mid-engined, large capacity supercar, the Diablo represented the last of a traditional breed.

1990 Honda NSX

The NSX was, in many ways, a very underrated supercar – and unique in this book for coming from Japan. Developed with the help of F1 legend Ayrton Senna, the NSX was Honda's attempt to spruce up its brand image. With the budget allocated to the project, Honda must have had the supercar

BELOW ***The Honda NSX scared the supercar establishment by combining high-tech engineering with the big budget of a huge car brand. Unfortunately, despite the car being hugely impressive, supercar buyers were not convinced.***

establishment worried. Made from aluminium, and with the first-ever use of variable valve timing on a road car, the NSX was crammed full of innovative features. Having been built in its own specially constructed factory, the NSX was easy to drive yet blisteringly fast. Ferrari's rival offering, the 348, seemed a slouch by comparison. F1 designer Gordon Murray was rumoured to drive his NSX almost daily. And, as Nick Mason told me, 'Everyone who is into supercars says it was so clever, it was ridiculous. I have never heard anyone say it was anything other than just totally brilliant.' And, certainly, Honda historians would suggest that the original NSX was so good, it forced Ferrari to up their game, resulting in the creation of the fabulous 355. Ultimately, public perception of Honda's brand proved too tricky to surmount, as customers opted instead for tried-and-tested supercar pedigrees, resulting in only modest sales of the NSX. However, a new Honda NSX Acura, with hybrid technology and slated for production from 2015 onwards, is hugely anticipated.

1991 Bugatti EB110

Bugatti might be best known in the modern era for the all-conquering Veyron, but back in 1991 the marque had lain dormant since 1962. Bugatti's long-standing reputation for cars of exceptional beauty, such as the Atlantic and Royale, had sadly become just a distant chapter in the history books. Bugattis were for museums, not roads.

Then, in the late 1980s, Italian entrepreneur Romano Artioli revitalised the marque and created a car so impressive and so crammed with new technology that it could be considered a candidate for inclusion in my Top Ten of game changers. That car was the Bugatti EB110.

'Artioli: A great character, a great gentleman but what a task!' enthused Bugatti historian Julius Kruta, when I asked him about the Italian-made predecessor to the Veyron. 'Artioli fulfilled his dream of building a Bugatti in Italy, in that Bermuda triangle around Modena where Ferrari, Lamborghini, Maserati and now Pagani and others reside.'

Artioli bought the Bugatti name and built a stunning factory near Modena, with the intention of building the most technically advanced supercar ever. This was a tall order, perhaps, but one that he (arguably) achieved when you read the spec sheet of the EB110. The car had many similarities to the eventual Veyron – including the first-ever use of a carbon-fibre monocoque chassis (originally developed on French space rockets), a speed-sensitive rear wing for high-speed driving, four-wheel drive, four turbos, a sub-four-second 0–60mph sprint time, a top speed of 212mph, as well as an extreme version called a Super Sport (producing 611bhp). Even the 'standard' V12, 3.5-litre, 60-valve engine was capable of 553bhp. The EB110 had supercar scissor doors thrown into the bargain. This was also a surprisingly dinky supercar – smaller than a Ferrari 348, in fact. And who did Artioli commission to design the EB110's show-stopping shell? Gandini, of course: the man behind the Miura, Countach, Diablo and Stratos, among many others. The chief engineer of the Countach was also involved in the construction of the EB110. The interior was super, with wooden trim,

air-conditioning and lavish leather detailing. The price was pretty super, too – at £281,000 ($475,000) for a basic-specification version.

Launched in Paris in 1991, with a parade of classic Bugattis leading in convoy to a black tie ball at the Palace of Versailles, the car seemed to quickly attract celebrity buyers – Formula 1 racing driver Michael Schumacher was rumoured to be one owner.

Unfortunately, however, there were just not enough owners to stave off Bugatti's insolvency, which coincided with a global recession that made super-expensive supercars frightening, even for the globe's wealthy elite of petrol-heads. As a result, just 139 EB110s were built. Despite its commercial failure, however, the EB110 is worthy of note as a car that showcased a number of technologies now considered staple elements of any modern-day supercar. And for that, Artioli must be heartily applauded.

BELOW ***Despite commercial failure, the Bugatti EB110 clearly made an impact at a cultural level, as die-cast maker Bburago has sold nearly 200,000 scale models.***

GAME CHANGER

1992 McLaren F1

IN 1992, A RACING CAR MANUFACTURER RELEASED A VEHICLE that was so revolutionary, so far ahead of its competitors and so instantly legendary, it is hard to believe they had never before released a large-volume production car. It was the fastest car ever made, it accelerated quicker than anything on the planet and it was so vastly superior to every high-performance car ever built that it won Le Mans on its debut. This car was called the McLaren F1, and to many people it is the greatest supercar of all time.

In order to find out how and why this astonishing car came about, I travelled to the McLaren headquarters in Woking, England – a place

ABOVE ***For many, this is the greatest supercar of all time: the McLaren F1, seen here in its extreme GTR variant.***

LEFT The F1 was not, in actual fact, McLaren's first road car. During the 1967 Can-Am racing season, the company dominated the field with their M6 and Bruce McLaren toyed with making a road car from that racer. To that end, two road-going examples were made by Trojan, including one built for McLaren himself. However, the car was never put into series production. (A third, Works, car was tested as a prototype by Bruce). The M6GT (left) had gullwing doors and a large 5.7-litre engine by Chevrolet.

that adds a new definition to the word 'meticulous'. Home to the McLaren racing team, which has won multiple world championships from the 1960s onwards, the 'McLaren Technology Centre' is a precisely designed temple to motoring genius. Entering the building via countless door swipes and security card checks, you then walk underneath the building through a spotless white tunnel, akin to a corridor on the Millennium Falcon. You then enter a near-hidden circular elevator before zooming up one floor...it is at this point you realise the elevator is made of glass as, shooting up through the floor of the main atrium, you are met by some of the most remarkable and important cars in motorsport. It is a breathtaking entrance.

Checking in at the front desk, situated atop a suspended platform, I sign in and wait for my host, a New Zealander named Keith Holland who has worked in both the McLaren F1 team and McLaren automotive businesses. Keith arrives bang on time, pristinely presented, and proceeds to give me a detailed tour of the building, paying special attention to the glittering array of cars on the floor below. As I walk alongside him to the downstairs area, I think I catch a glimpse of a familiar-looking silhouette out of the corner of my eye...

Keith is a hugely amiable and massively experienced part of the McLaren team, having worked on various F1-winning cars, among other triumphs. With great passion, he tells me about a particular Ayrton Senna McLaren and the incredible Can-Am car driven by Bruce McLaren himself, as well as a host of other historically significant vehicles. Then, I find myself drawn to two cars in the corner, set alongside each other: a pair of McLaren F1 road cars. Their charisma is tangible.

Keith is visibly proud as he talks to me about the two F1s and is fired up by the F1 LM example (one of only five). As we chat about the cars, with Keith's encyclopaedic knowledge only matched by his passion for McLaren, I am enthralled by the remarkable story of this game-changing supercar.

By the late 1980s, the supercar world had been drawn into a peculiar automotive arms race, with the Porsche 959 and Ferrari F40 starting a competition among manufacturers to boast the fastest acceleration and highest top speed. McLaren's race team watched on, slightly bemused but also intrigued. According to legend, a number of McLaren engineers were sitting in the departure lounge of Milan airport in 1988 and talking about this situation, when the idea was mooted to make, quite simply, the greatest supercar – indeed the greatest car of any kind – the world had ever seen.

The brains behind the plan were all genuine motoring luminaries: Gordon Murray was a former prodigious engineer for the Brabham and McLaren F1 teams; Peter Stevens was a designer for, among other classics, the recent Lotus Elan as well as the XJR-15 Jaguar; and, of course, there was Ron Dennis, the exacting champion of the whole organisation. Their combined ambition was irresistible, and so, the project was green-lighted with a 'no expenses spared' approach to creating what would be the absolute pinnacle of automotive design.

The machine they would create was to be so far ahead of its rivals, so utterly superior to any of its contemporaries, that it was almost hard to comprehend. And, indeed, the F1 would set a benchmark that was untouchable for well over a decade. Overnight, every other supercar seemed almost obsolete. So, how did McLaren do this?

BELOW ***The McLaren Technology Centre in Woking, England – a temple of precision.***

Dennis and Murray are both renowned for their obsessive attention to detail. And this was apparent in every single element of the F1 project, right from the now-legendary ten-hour initial briefing that Murray gave to his team. The car was to be ultra-light – ideally less than 1,000kg – using only the finest components. It would utilise as much F1 technology as possible with the aim of being the fastest and the very best on the planet. Murray had three main ambitions for the car: first, to solve the classic supercar problems such as bad visibility, poor seating position and positioning of pedals, lack of luggage space, poor stereos and air-conditioning; second, to enhance the driving experience, prioritising that over all else; and, finally, to have a centrally located driving position.

The development phase was painstaking, with the minutest of details pored over in acute focus. For Murray and Dennis, a flaw in the tiniest detail could let down the entire philosophy. Eventually, in May 1992, the McLaren F1 made its public debut in Monte Carlo, three days before that year's grand prix. Gordon Murray had said the creation would topple everything ever built before – he was unreservedly correct.

The F1's spec sheet is still staggering reading more than two decades after the car's launch. The engine was a mighty V12, designed especially by BMW Motorsport. The McLaren F1 was mid-engined, with a 6.1-litre and longitudinally mounted engine powering a rear-wheel drive, operated via a six-speed manual gearbox. Notably, and in contrast to so many of its competitors, there were no turbos, making this the most powerful normally aspirated engine ever seen at that time. The engine head and block were aluminium, but many smaller parts were made from magnesium, which is even lighter. This engine generated 627bhp, and a mind-blowing, record-setting 559bhp per tonne (a measurement that many petrol-heads feel is more indicative of a car's genuine, real-world power).

LEFT ***The F1's fabled engine bay cover was plated with gold leaf, as this was considered the best material for controlling temperature.***

RIGHT ***The McLaren F1 – in many people's opinion, the greatest supercar of all time.***

KENWOOD

LARK

This apocalyptic force propelled the F1 to world-record figures that were so far ahead of the competition, it was almost laughable. Sixty miles per hour could be reached in 3.2 seconds, 100 in just 6.3 seconds, and with a top speed of 231mph (later extended to 242mph), no other car even came close.

The timeless bodywork, created by Peter Stevens, perfectly complemented the engineering genius beneath. Since Murray had created a long wheelbase with a subsequent low centre of gravity, there was minimal front or rear overhang, making the F1 a very compact car, with only a very modest footprint. This made a mockery of goliath supercars, such as the massive Ferrari Testarossa. The side strakes flowed sinuously, and the scoop intake on the roof funnelled air into the massive engine while also looking fabulous. It has been said that the F1 continues to look like a brand-new design, and there is some resonance in that.

Underneath the all-carbon-fibre bodywork lay a carbon-fibre chassis. Such materials might be commonplace now, but in 1992, such extensive use was almost unheard of. The F1 boasted a carbon-fibre monocoque using F1 technology, reinforced with aluminium honeycomb panels and Kevlar. An aluminium- and honeycomb-structured Nomex core was overlaid with 94 panels of composite material, in a meticulously slow and precise construction process. As a result, each car took around one month to produce, with the carbon fibre alone taking 400-plus man hours. Such generous use of composite materials pegged the F1 to just 1,140kg – only slightly more than Murray's goal of 1,000kg. Putting that in context, this means that the F1 is a quarter of a tonne lighter than an ultra-light Porsche 911 GT3RS.

The undertray was inspired by McLaren's racing expertise to hold the car to the ground with aerodynamic features such as rear diffusers. The F1 was fitted with two fans to remove 'boundary air', which would have made the car twitchy at the rear (a system directly inspired by Murray's 1978 Brabham F1 cars). The idea was that rather than have aerofoils and spoilers to push the car down on to the road, clever F1-inspired technology would suck it down instead. There was just one spoiler, which popped up under heavy braking for extra control. Other racing-inspired elements included a fuel cell (rather than tank), an ultra-complex exhausts system that looked more like a work of art and a three-plate carbon-on-carbon clutch.

This meant there was, then, plenty of power to make the F1 accelerate, and so McLaren did not skimp on the stopping power, either. Magnesium-alloy race-style wheels were initially intended to have carbon brakes, but that technology was not practical for road use at the time. Instead, Murray installed intelligent brake cooling: a system whereby small ducts only opened when the brakes needed extra cooling, thus minimising unnecessary drag. This is another example of the car's supreme intelligence, which led renowned American supercar expert John Lamm to call the F1 'the Einstein of the exotics'.

Make no mistake: the 'no money no object' approach to making the very finest car ever built did not equate to randomly throwing technology

ABOVE ***The McLaren F1 held the record for the fastest production car in the world for many years. The F1 that was piloted to a 243mph world record by Andy Wallace was called the XP5.***

at the F1. To keep the driving experience as pure and unadulterated as possible, Murray insisted on no traction control, no hydraulic steering assistance/power steering, no anti-lock brakes and not even a brake servo. This had the added bonus of also saving weight. When people mocked the rather feeble-sounding horn, McLaren explained that a louder air horn was not used because it was considered too heavy.

The F1 has unique forward-pivoting scissor doors, known as 'dihedral', which are opened by pushing a button on the rear wing, slinging them upwards and forwards in a very dramatic process. Another utterly unique

RIGHT **I wish I owned this number plate.**

feature of the McLaren F1 is the fact that it has three seats, with the driver centrally located, slightly ahead of the two side passengers. This was intended to mimic a single-seater race car in terms of position and visibility. Of course, this required a fairly adventurous journey into the driver's seat, but once you were there it made perfect sense. Having been lucky enough to go out in a particular rock star's F1 in the mid-1990s, I can also testify that at very high speed (70mph, plus ten per cent, of course), the right-hand passenger seat feels scarily close to oncoming traffic.

The interior was clean and simple but expensively appointed: Nardi steering wheel, Connolly leather upholstery, air-conditioning, electric windows and a high-end Kenwood CD player (no radio), of which Murray – a serious music lover – was very proud. Even here, he demanded that the CD player be lightweight, less than 20lb. Steering wheel, pedals and seats were all custom-fitted to each owner. A large, red starter button was the suitable race car way to bring the beast to life, complete with fighter jet safety cover. The foot pedals were exquisitely machined in aluminium, each emblazoned with the F1 logo.

However, this was no track car for the playboy. Murray was very keen for the F1 to be docile around town and useable every day. He wanted owners of an F1 to be able to go away for the weekend in his car – hence, the inclusion of clever custom luggage that stowed away in compartments just ahead of the rear wheels. There were other clever extras, too, such as high-end Facom titanium tool kits (one for the car and a larger box set for garage mechanics), a custom car cover, a gold-plated engine bay to protect the carbon fibre from heat and engine diagnostics via a telephone link-up anywhere in the world.

Along with the previously mentioned rock star's F1, I was also fortunate enough to be (slightly) involved in the purchase of a very early chassis F1 for a friend who had made his fortune in the retail industry. A few weeks after paying almost double the cost for an early chassis than for a normal F1, my friend rang with a question. He wanted to know if it was okay that his dad had gone to Sainsbury's in the McLaren. If that doesn't meet Murray's 'usability' criteria, then what does?

One of the F1's most remarkable achievements (among many), is that of Le Mans. When McLaren decided to go racing (after several customers had urged them to do so), on its Le Mans debut in 1995, the F1 came 1st, 3rd, 4th and 5th and 13th, with one car hitting 198mph during the race. This was the first time since the 1940s that Le Mans had been won by a road car. To celebrate, McLaren built five ultra-rare, orange-liveried versions, known as the LM (each of which is now highly valuable). These were even more powerful than the racer, with an incredible 668bhp. There was also an F1 GTR, which was also hugely successful in the GT series.

Of course, all this didn't come cheap. On its launch, the F1 cost £635,000 (well over $1 million). To provide some context, that was half a million pounds more than some Ferraris. The first F1 was delivered to a customer in January 1994, with initial plans to build 300 cars. These targets were ultimately scaled back, and a final run of 106 was completed (including

McLaren F1

LAUNCHED

1992

POWER

627bhp

ACCELERATION

0–60mph in 3.2 secs

MAXIMUM SPEED

231mph (later extended to 242mph)

PRODUCTION RUN

The initial plan was to build 300 cars, but ultimately just 106 were completed.

the 'standard' F1, LM, GT, GTR and prototypes). The F1's rarity – along with its legend – has meant that it remains one of the most valuable cars ever built.

The McLaren F1 was the undisputed king of all supercars for over a decade, its top speed so far in excess of its rivals that most manufacturers simply gave up trying to compete. While other supercar prices fluctuate, F1 values seem to just keep increasing, with LM models rumoured to be worth in excess of £20 million ($34 million). This last point returns me to the two F1s at Woking that day, as I stand there with Keith, surveying that famous bodywork. 'Some car, eh?' said Keith, smiling cheekily at the nature of his understatement.

It is a mark of the F1's genius that it took £1.5 billion ($2.5 billion) of VW Group's finest engineering brains to create the Bugatti Veyron before the McLaren F1 finally surrendered its performance crown. The F1 changed the game in so many ways – the materials it used, the performance figures it generated, the impact it had on the wider philosophy of supercars – that some consider it to be the absolute best of all time. In any dream garage of supercars, the first name on many people's list would be the glorious F1.

ABOVE ***The McLaren F1's Le Mans debut was historically significant, as it was the first road car to win there since the 1940s.***

1992 Jaguar XJ220

The 1990s claimed more than just the Bugatti EB110 as a victim of the recession: the Jaguar XJ220 was another very high-profile casualty – although its failure wasn't just due to the economic downturn. Launched in 1991, the initial plan was the result of after-hours meetings of elite Jaguar engineers (calling themselves 'The Saturday Club') – a reassuringly purist beginning to the car's life. The plan was to create the world's fastest car, with a top speed of 220mph (hence the name). There was also talk of the car competing in the Group B races that spawned both the Ferrari 288GTO and Porsche 959.

The 1988 concept version of the XJ220 shown at the Birmingham Motor Show made arguably the biggest impact at any British show in car history. The proposed car offered Porsche 959-like technology, including a 6.2-litre, V12, 48-valve mid-engined power plant, with four-wheel drive, forward-tilting doors and adaptive suspension. In the late 1980s, supercar business was booming, so the timing seemed perfect for this genuine British sensation. However, one year later, Ford took over Jaguar and that ambition seemed to slip out of the programme. The eventual production car was somewhat less inspiring, with standard doors, a rather agricultural-

BELOW ***Perhaps Jaguar XJ220 customers wished they had bought the 1992 Jaguar XJR-15 instead: a road-going version of the Le Mans-winning car. With a V12 monster of an engine, easily capable of passing 200mph, the car nonetheless cost more than £500,000 ($840,000).***

sounding 3.5-litre V6 and conventional suspension. Admittedly, the new car included twin turbos (a first for Jaguar) that helped produce 542bhp, but it was rear-wheel drive only. The lightweight, bonded-honeycomb, aluminium body was one of its technological highlights, along with a racing fuel cell and the amazingly sleek body design, which is still a massive head turner. This styling cleverly drew its inspiration from the D-Type and old XJ13 racing Jaguars. In keeping with Jaguar tradition, the interior was rather sumptuous – rich leather seats, air-conditioning, electric windows, a six-CD stereo and a glass roof for light. This was all most 'un-supercar-ish' when compared to the race-wannabes of the previous decade, leading one reviewer to call the XJ220 a 'supercar limo'.

Unfortunately, along with delays, the price kept rising and ended up as double that of a Ferrari F40, as it eventually reached £403,000 ($680,000). Combine that with the global recession at the time and a rash of cancelled orders, as well as legal letters from disgruntled customers, and you can see why the XJ220 became another high-profile supercar casualty. Ultimately, only around 275 cars were built. This commercial failure is a shame when you consider, as some reviewers have, that objectively speaking the car is a hugely capable machine – in fact, it held the Nürburgring production car lap record for an amazing eight years.

1995 Ferrari F50

With the F40 created to celebrate the great Italian marque's fortieth birthday, the supercar world looked on with anticipation when the same brand approached 50. And, sure enough (following suit of other leading supercars of the time), Ferrari announced that the next hypercar from Maranello – the F50 – had the central premise of being the closest experience to an F1 car for the road.

And there were to be plenty of elements in the F50's make-up that suggested this was exactly what you would get for the half-a-million-dollar price tag. The engine was based on the 1990s series of F1 cars, as driven by Alain Prost (the power unit was also found in an altered form in the successful 333SP American racer). The engine was normally aspirated, unlike the turbo F40, and enlarged to a 4.7-litre, 520bhp V12, making it the most powerful non-turbo engine of the day (in 1995, turbos were banned in F1). Due to concerns about reliability, the F1 paddle shift was not used in the F50. Instead, a classic six-speed manual box was offered.

The F1 connections didn't stop there. Ferrari commissioned their F1 brake supplier Brembo to produce the massive brakes used for the F50. With the racing connection in mind, there was no ABS, and the brakes were not assisted in any way, matching an F1 car. The chassis, too, was the stuff of the race track. Using Kevlar, Nomex and carbon fibre, the extremely light but exceptionally strong monocoque tub weighed just 224lb. The same use of composite materials sheathed the spectacular bodywork, making the car's kerb weight just 1,350kg.

There was more: the F50 had no petrol tank, but instead a fuel cell made from rubber, again as per F1. The aerodynamics of the bodywork had been designed in a wind tunnel, which can easily be seen when looking at the car's sweeping lines. Again F1 influenced, the suspension was electronically controlled, using pushrods and rockers. Additionally, in a direct nod to Prost's F1 car, the suspension was attached directly to the chassis, as was the steering, which made for a very loud ride. Finally, the F50 had the very first use of real-time telemetry inside a road-going car.

The car was visually softer than the angular Ferrari F40, but it still presented a striking red arrow. Early drawings drew on the stunning 1989 Ferrari Mythos show car, and both cars share the roofless approach – again designed to mimic the open cockpit of an F1 car. Ferrari had Pininfarina design the bodywork, which looks notably more exciting in the flesh than in photos, especially the huge, oversized rear spoiler (which helped create sublime handling). Finally, massive cooling scoops in the nose and bonnet gave the F50 a very distinct, almost cartoonish look.

Getting in to an F50 was always a bit of a spectacle, thanks to a high sill, which meant you flopped down into the car rather ungraciously. The minimalist interior was deliberately sparse – though disappointingly so, perhaps, when you think of the price tag. Generous use of carbon fibre extended to the gear knob and interior panels, while the thin seats and lack of carpets aped the F40. The F50 was not famously comfortable and was certainly not quiet, either, with that monstrous V12 howling right behind the driver's head. The squishy rubber starter button seemed oddly low-tech and in contrast to the electronic LCD displays (unique from previous road Ferraris but as per current F1 cars). There were customer complaints about the cabin overheating, even with air-conditioning as standard. Storage space was enough for a few sunglasses,

BELOW ***The F50 was a technological statement from Ferrari, crammed with F1 technology and heavily influenced by the genius of F1 World Champion Michael Schumacher.***

perhaps, but that was about it. There was no stereo system (probably because it would have been impossible to hear, anyway).

The number of F50s built was dictated by an old Ferrari adage: always build one fewer than you think you can sell. Thus, 349 F50s rolled off the specially designated production line in the Maranello factory. For the super-rich collector, it is worth knowing that three F50 GTs were built using lighter panels and delivering 750bhp. But Ferrari canned that racing ambition so it could concentrate on its F1 programme (with pretty good results, it must be said, as Michael Schumacher scooped seven world titles). Ferrari said that future legislation would prevent them ever again making a two-seater F1 car homologated for the road like the F50. The entire production run only lasted two years, and this time, unlike with the extended run for the F40, the final total was delivered, as promised, at 349 cars.

The F50 was a viciously fast Ferrari – faster than the beloved F40, in fact. However, it was also more refined to drive, which didn't go down well with purists still in love with the rawness of its fortieth-anniversary predecessor. Even with no ABS, traction control, four-wheel drive or power-assisted steering, it still felt cosseted by comparison. The F50 suffered from the sheer brilliance of the F40's legacy and was overshadowed by such a landmark car, and, so always struggled to create its own legend. The F50 never raced and didn't set any new performance benchmarks. It was also completely in the shadow of the stunning McLaren F1 (which was twice the price, although no one seemed to care), so the F50 struggles to find favour among many supercar connoisseurs. But perhaps history will judge it more kindly as it really is an incredible piece of kit!

BELOW ***The Ferrari F50 always struggled against the reputation of its predecessor, the mighty F40. Although the F50 was technologically superior, the general consensus was that the F40 was a purer and more coherent Ferrari.***

GAME CHANGER

1999 Pagani Zonda

THE JOE MACARI SHOWROOM IN SOUTH LONDON, ENGLAND is a gleaming, spectacularly designed temple to supercar religion. In sharp contrast to the pitch-black winter night outside, the ultra-bright lights inside illuminate a collection of cars that are rarely seen together. Macari is unveiling his first showroom, and now the great and the good of the British supercar world have descended here for a launch party. Macari is a racing driver as well as a genius restorer of early Ferraris who has become one of the leading lights of the British supercar market, and, so, when he opens a showroom, *everyone* turns up.

ABOVE ***Each Zonda came with its own bespoke luggage and a pair of custom-made driving shoes.***

As fascinating as the people-watching at this launch might promise to be, though, I am not here for that. I am here by the good grace of Dominik Amian, another one-time-racer, and my eyes are drawn instantly to the list of genuine game-changing supercars on show, which is just ridiculous. On the far wall are four sparkling-red Ferraris laid out in sequence: 288GTO, F40, F50, Enzo. Across the way is a golden Bugatti Veyron. And not far from there sit both a Lamborghini Miura and McLaren F1. Here, 1950s racing Ferraris mingle with GT racers, parked next to vintage Mercedes. This is illustrious company: the sort of company where it takes a truly astonishing car to stand out.

And that, I am sure, is exactly what the crowd huddled around the Pagani Zonda are thinking. Despite the stunning array of supercars under

BELOW ***The Pagani Zonda was a shock to the supercar establishment: the manifestation of a very personal and passionate philosophy and absolutely a game changer in the market.***

this one roof on this evening, I am repeatedly struck by the amount of attention the Zonda receives. Time and again people kneel down to inspect the carbon-fibre cabin and walk around the rear to see those incredible exhausts and wide, muscular hindquarters. They take photos. They talk about it. And, in my opinion, their interest is well deserved. For that reason, the Pagani Zonda is my eighth game changer.

Launched in 1999, the Zonda began deliveries in 2000 and the world was instantly astonished. Within ten years, Pagani had become an established name in the market. In the history of supercars, how many times has that happened?

The story of the Zonda is inextricably linked to the tale of Horacio Pagani. Like Ettore Bugatti, Ferdinand Porsche and Enzo Ferrari before him, Horacio Pagani's personality and personal vision has shaped the cars he makes more than any design studio ever could. The son of a baker, Horacio was born in Casilda, Argentina. As a kid, he would draw cars and then started making models of his designs from balsa wood. By the age of 16, he was designing and building Mini Motos. During his diploma at technical school, Pagani constructed a small buggy car, before going on to study industrial design and then mechanical engineering at university. In his early twenties, he designed a complete single-seater F2 car, before starting to work with fibreglass for use on pick-up trucks.

Deciding to move to Italy, Pagani took with him a letter of recommendation from Argentinian racing legend, Juan Manuel Fangio, to help him get work. He duly got a job at Lamborghini, where he soon became known for his deep understanding of carbon-fibre materials. At this time, he worked on the beginnings of the Diablo and also on the 25th anniversary edition of the Countach.

Then, in 1991, Pagani set up his own factory specialising in composites in Modena, right in the backyard of Ferrari and Lamborghini. He made composite parts for numerous companies, including the Ferrari F1 team. Soon, his factory was so successful that he began to have the financial clout to think about building his own supercar. Once he began developing the Zonda, Horacio personally drew the exterior, the tub, the chassis and suspension, among other elements, drawing them with an old-fashioned draughtsman's board and pencil. Of course, those drawings were then handed over to his designers' computers, but the original inspiration was all hand-drawn. It was to be a full eight years later that Horacio revealed his first car at the 1999 Geneva Motor Show.

Instantly, the Zonda looked insanely 'special', with its forward-flung cabin and muscular rear rising up to grab the road. (The later race versions looked even more spectacular.) Of course, Horacio drew the silhouette himself, and, with the Zonda, he just got the design *right*.

The Zonda's central structure has an aluminium subframe, but pretty much everything else is carbon fibre. As a result, the bodywork weighs just 136lb. The use of carbon fibre isn't just to make the car light, however, as is the case with the Ferrari F40. Rather, the bodywork and interior are exquisitely crafted into automotive art. All of the seams align at every single point. This is some achievement if you consider that they are made from thousands of tiny squares of carbon fibre wrapped around curved, three-dimensional shapes such as a steering wheel. It has been said that Pagani's carbon-fibre workshop is more like a Saville Row tailors than a car factory, and that is perhaps why many Pagani customers have their cars in bare exposed carbon finish.

However, it isn't just the carbon fibre that has this level of detail: each weld is so tiny and tight, it is like a slight pencil line. Every washer, nut, bolt and part has been pored over and designed to be a work of art in its own right. One wheel hub took more than a year to perfect. Pagani's logo is often carved into the tiniest of the 4,000-plus pieces that make each car. If you read an interview with Horacio Pagani, you are as likely to hear about art, philosophy, science and beauty, as you are about horsepower or torque. He is fascinated by Leonardo Da Vinci and calls the factory, which he personally designed, an atelier ('workshop'), and he lives...well, he lives on site. All this is the actual practice of the epiphany Pagani had when he read Da Vinci's belief that 'art and science can go hand in hand.' Nowhere is this more apparent than in the Zonda's cabin, which is like sitting in a jewellery store: the dials and switches appearing like precious stones. The round pedals look like sculptures. It is just stunning.

John Morrison works at Macari's showroom and previously raced successfully for various manufacturers (sufficient to earn him a BRDC Membership). John followed this with management-level sales work for the likes of Porsche, McLaren, Lamborghini, Bugatti and Ferrari (both manufacturers and retailers), finishing with three years with Horacio Pagani. So, he is more qualified than most to comment on why the Zonda has made such an impact. 'It makes a wonderful noise, and it is a wonderful place to sit: you are low down, so you really do feel like you're in a race car, yet you can drive it easily. The clutch is gentle; it doesn't bite you as you move away.'

The Zonda is not all flair, however. The 7.3-litre, 600bhp, V12 engine was made by AMG and has a manual gearbox. No turbos. Its sound is quite incredible. Most Zonda owners leave the window down before they start

BELOW ***The Zonda's interior is a masterpiece of carbon-fibre craftsmanship.***

RIGHT ***The Zonda was available in a dazzling array of one-offs and limited editions: the S, the F (F for Fangio), the R, the Cinque, the Tricolore. All included evolved versions of the V12 and individual design tweaks – advances that the debut car was easily able to incorporate.***

LEFT ***The wide, muscular rear of a Zonda is a striking angle from which to look at this incredible new supercar.***

up so they can hear the roar of the engine. The mechanics are very direct, analogue – you could say old-school – with a normal clutch and rear-wheel drive: mechanical simplicity that is in sharp contrast to the complex design and interior. However, this keeps the Zonda as a pure driver's supercar. At the same time, as John Morrison says, the Zonda is renowned for being relatively easy to drive: this is no Ferrari F40 or Porsche Carrera GT.

'There is little doubt,' continues John, 'that it is a pretty remarkable piece of work. It was Horatio's first independent production car. So, bearing in mind that he had not made a car before, it is absolutely remarkable. It is fundamentally user-friendly, even though it can look rather angry and mean and a handful. It works so well and you get in it and just relax. You are aware you are in something completely competent. That is to do with pedal weights, with balanced responses, with so many things being tactile and straightforward. That is incredibly hard to create.'

'Horacio was brought up in the Italian motoring world, and so he had a very good feel for what wealthy people enjoyed in terms of materials and finishes. In that sense, he is an absolute genius. He has kept models of all the things that he loved as a youngster. He keeps them and is still inspired by them. His cerebral approach to the business of car design and manufacture is as much about philosophy as anything else. The factory is also an essential part of the story; they are lovely people making works of art and nothing is allowed to stand in the way of that, certainly not timetables, processes or anything like that.'

It could be argued that the Zonda was the first supercar to really properly use carbon fibre. Previous supercars had used carbon fibre, of course, many times, yet perhaps the Zonda was the first car to *feel* the carbon fibre. 'He was grappling with carbon fibre from a very early point in its use,' explains John, 'yet now he really has mastered the art. That is central to how the Zonda has changed the game. Also, the sheer attention to detail is staggering: the quality of the components, *every single component*, and the quality of the end result.'

BELOW ***The all-black, all-carbon Zonda R was a race car that was not eligible for competition but nor was it road legal, either. So, in effect, the owner would need a private race track to use it.***

Eventually, Horacio made 130 Zondas. With those cars, he established Pagani as a new supercar force. Dozens of companies have tried to achieve the same; some would argue, only Pagani has succeeded. For that reason, as well as its world-leading use of carbon fibre, the Zonda is an absolute game changer.

For Horacio Pagani, a supercar has to evoke emotion. Standing next to the Zonda on that night at Joe Macari's showroom, watching the throng of people look in awe, I could see he had done exactly that. At least as many people kept returning to look at the Zonda as any of the other specimens of supercar royalty in that pristine showroom.

Towards the end of the evening, I started chatting to an immaculately dressed man standing near the Zonda. It turned out this was his car. I asked him why he loved the Pagani so much. 'It's normally aspirated, manual gearbox, seven litres. I can take it around town and it performs fine, or I can do 200mph on the autobahn and it's fine. It is very comfortable: Horacio used to have a very bad back, so when he designed the car, he bore that in mind. I like the idea of the exclusivity of it. There's a family of Pagani owners and if you choose to buy one, they are more than happy to spend time with them. I'd looked for a while, I'd been out to see them and each time one came up and they said, "We don't know this car, it's never been back to the factory. We don't know anything about it; be patient." Eventually, they found a car for me. The Zonda is the one supercar I will never sell.'

Pagani Zonda

LAUNCHED

1999

POWER

The original model could power to 495bhp, while the later 7.3-litre, V12 engine edition was capable of 600bhp

ACCELERATION

0–62.5mph in 3.7 secs

MAXIMUM SPEED

214mph

PRODUCTION RUN

Just 130 Zondas have been made so far, with the final Zonda planned a circuit-only R-development: the 'Revolucione'.

Also in the 1990s

1991 Cizeta Moroder Designed by Countach/Miura/Diablo-man Gandini, the car is clearly genetically related to those famous Lamborghinis – at least visually.

1991 Alpine A610 The successor to the Renault Alpine GTA, it boasted an even bigger engine and turbo charging. Although the 610 bore a strong resemblance to the GTA (due to limited development budgets at the time), the car was a comprehensive evolution. Its commercial success was muted, but the car found favour among the press and public alike. To this day, there is a fanatical and loyal fan-base for this unheralded but worthy French entry.

1993 Lister Storm The Storm was British tuning company Lister's first attempt at their own supercar. They certainly had the right idea – a 7-litre, V12 engine based on the Jaguar XJR Le Mans-winning power unit, creating 546bhp and good for 208mph. The project was commercially very challenging for the brand, and so only a handful were built.

1993 De Tomaso Guara The marque's final car, named after a South American wolf. The Guara made clever use of Kevlar and fibreglass.

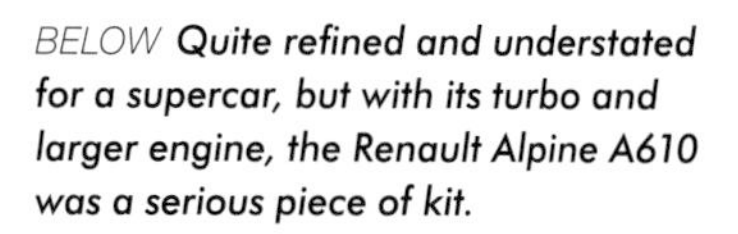
BELOW ***Quite refined and understated for a supercar, but with its turbo and larger engine, the Renault Alpine A610 was a serious piece of kit.***

1994 Ferrari 355 The first Ferrari to have a semi-automatic paddle shift, the 355 has an absolutely classic silhouette that is seen by many as one of the great modern Ferrari shapes. The car is also famously easy to use and drive.

1995 Venturi 400GT This was a limited-edition road car also used for racing. With a twin-turbo, 3-litre V6, it was good for 400bhp, and the carbon ceramic brakes were an early use of race technology on a road car.

ABOVE AND LEFT ***The Ferrari 355 is one of the marque's finest silhouettes: easy to drive and yet still devastatingly swift. It is a great modern Ferrari.***

RIGHT *Not exactly an F40 for looks, but the Ferrari 550 Maranello was an impressive piece of engineering.*

BELOW RIGHT *The Ultima GTR was a race car made road legal. Stunning to look at and with record-breaking performance.*

BELOW *The TVR Cerbera was a four-wheeled ballistic missile from Blackpool, England. Its name is derived from Cerberus, a three-headed monster of Greek mythology that stood guard over the entrance of Hades...rather than Blackpool.*

1996 Ferrari 550 Maranello The Maranello was, notably, front-engined but still remained a great supercar.

1996 TVR Cerbera Briefly the fastest production car in the world, with low-slung looks and a gorgeous engine note from TVR's first in-house power plant (a V8), the Cerbera was a deceptively mad supercar. The Cerbera's brutal acceleration could be twitchy and so was best handled with care. Several models were plagued with reliability issues, but this was, nonetheless, a genuine supercar baiter. The even-more striking TVR Tuscan was similarly quick off the mark, while the Speed 12 one-off was basically a Cerbera with two V6s wedged under the bonnet, providing 900bhp, from 7.7 litres, in a car weighing less than 1,000kg. Given that, probably not an everyday car, then!

1999 Ultima GTR Available in kit form or pre-built by the company, the Ultima GTR has acceleration faster than any Ferrari ever built and holds numerous acceleration world records (for example, 0–100mph in 5.8 seconds). The GTR offered hypercar performance for the price of a standard Porsche 911. The car is actually rather petite, yet has a striking road presence because of the exaggerated scoops and dips. Its small size helps its ultra-light total weight, which makes this pretty much a road-going ballistic missile. The Ultima GTR can get to 60mph quicker than a Ferrari F40. That's food for thought.

What about?

Here is a selection of really significant cars that are worthy of further investigation. They might not be game changers, or even the most high-profile cars of their era, but the following list deserves special mention.

1991 LCC Rocket – pioneer car for a generation of track-day open-seaters
1991 Westfield SEight
1992 Vector WX-3
1994 Marcos LM 500
1994 Venturi Atlantique and **400GT**
1998 Dare DZ
1998 Mercedes-Benz CLK GTR
1998 Ascari Ecosse
1999 TVR Tuscan

The 2000s and Onwards

LEFT ***A one-off, this Enzo-based hypercar was made in collaboration with American collector James Glickenhuas. The project was so successful that Ferrari decided to badge it as a genuine Ferrari, calling it the Ferrari P4/5 by Pininfarina. This car has been dubbed 'The Beast of Turin'.***

By the turn of the century, the evolution of supercars had reached such a peak that the ability to 'change the game' was becoming increasingly rare. And by the end of 2010, this was even more so. As an example, gear shift times had been reduced to being effectively instantaneous, with some manufacturers even building in a slight 'clunk' to make the driver feel more engaged. Likewise, the mid-engine layout, which had long since been proven the optimal placement for a supercar's engine, was now largely universal. Performance figures were also narrowing in terms of margins of improvement – after all, there is only so much faster you can go than 60mph in under three seconds. Launch acceleration was reaching such peaks that it was becoming more to do with grip than it was power and torque. Even the old supercar white elephant – terrible fuel consumption – was being addressed.

Back in 1954, the Mercedes-Benz Gullwing shocked the world with its looks. In 1966, it was enough for the Miura to be a pivotal game changer (or game starter) by simply putting the engine in the middle of the car. Introducing outlandish looks (Lamborghini Countach) or high technology (Porsche 959) was also once enough, as were ever-higher top speeds (Ferrari F40) or new materials (McLaren F1), and so on. In the 21st century, however, supercar manufacturers have all that history to contend with: so much has been done before that the precedents are enormous.

On the surface, this fact should be very intimidating to supercar manufacturers. And yet, when it came to writing this chapter, it was fascinating and exciting to find that, compared to previous decades, my research simply demanded that I include material on a much larger number of key cars. Supercar makers have today evolved their craft to such a refined degree that this chapter necessarily has to include details of many more cars than the previous decades. This, in itself, is indicative of the fact that rather than becoming the dinosaurs of an old era that doom-mongers predicted, supercars are in fact as essential and popular now as they have ever been.

As a consequence of more than half a century of supercar evolution, we may not now be able to witness so many game changers. However, the upside of this historical fact is that the overall excellence of supercars has been raised to a staggering level. It is now simply not acceptable to have poor gear shifts, shoddy interiors, unduly noisy cabins and badly finished bodywork. To enter the supercar market in the new century, you pretty much have to get absolutely everything right. And, as you will see from this chapter, so many manufacturers are doing exactly that.

2002 Enzo Ferrari

When Ferrari announced that they were making a new hypercar in memory of their late founder, the watching world knew the stakes were high. This had to be nothing less than the greatest Ferrari ever built. At the time, the brand's F1 team was dominating every race, with Michael Schumacher on his way to seven world titles. And, with the German racing legend on board for development of this new car, the timing seemed perfect.

To begin with, the early design drawings released for the Enzo weren't exciting people and looked too much like a Le Mans racer. So, super-talented Pininfarina designer Ken Okuyama drew his idea for the car over the course of an inspired lunchbreak – sketching an F1 car first, then drawing light pencil lines of bodywork over that basic shape. Ferrari didn't want lots of extraneous wings and spoilers, but they did want more than 200mph. Consequently, the car spent an age in wind tunnels, where numerous crucial scoops and vents were added, which benefitted the look as well as the performance.

Based on early press shots, initial reaction to the new car's shape was not always positive and there was quite some controversy surrounding the car before its launch (later, one business magazine placed it as one of 'The Ugliest Cars of the Past Fifty Years'). Originally, the roof was intended to be black, so that when you looked down on the Enzo, it had the appearance of an F1 car. There were also two development noses: an F1 shape and a more 'normal' shape. The manufacturer waited until a day after it had won its fourth consecutive constructor's championship and then went with the F1-inspired nose.

When the car was finally launched, in 2002, it was dripping with F1 technology. The V12, 6-litre, 650bhp, ultra-lightweight aluminium engine was the first of a new generation and boasted a world-leading electronic engine control system, feeding power to the rear wheels only. The Enzo had a 218mph top speed, making it the fastest Ferrari ever (and with a 0–60mph time of 3.3 seconds). As in F1 at the time, there were no turbos, and the car had the world's first use of carbon-ceramic brakes in a road car, complete with ABS. The chassis was carbon fibre, weighing just 202lb. Even the dramatic scissor doors felt light to open (albeit no longer revolutionary in their composition). Everything about the car was light but super strong. One Enzo crashed at 125mph into a telegraph pole and was cut in half, but the tub worked to perfection and the driver walked away with only a bloody lip.

So-called 'adaptive aero' had been banned from F1, but the Enzo used this aerodynamics technology to create further downforce and grip. (There are even flaps hidden within the nose, which manipulate the flow of air to aid cooling and downforce.) A small rear wing rises at 37mph to further enhance the aerodynamics, before lowering again for high speeds. There is also a flat undertray with a so-called venturi, which sucked the car

BELOW ***In 2004, the Enzo Ferrari became the subject of eBay's most expensive ever car bid, with one selling for £544,000 ($920,000). Elsewhere, a survey revealed that 86% of men would rather spend the weekend with an Enzo than with Pamela Anderson!***

RIGHT ***The Enzo Ferrari.***

down on to the ground – again, drawing on F1 technology. The suction is so strong that when following an Enzo, you can visibly see dirt being sucked up off the road. (The car would also be hoovering up money, however, as fuel consumption could be as low as single figures!)

During the development process, Michael Schumacher had evolved some of the most cutting-edge computer technology for the car and much of this made its way into the cabin. There were F1-style control buttons on the steering wheel, launch control, as well as a strip of red LED lights along the top of the wheel for the rev counter. A high-tech ASR traction control system and ultra-fast, F1-style, six-speed paddle shift completed the stellar array. For some purists, the extravagance of all this technology became an issue; complaints about abrupt shifting were not uncommon, and one owner I met complained that he was frustrated by the sense of so many computers being between him and the road (this gripe was ultimately the reason why he traded his Enzo in for an F40).

Ferrari planned to make just 399 cars (all of which were pre-sold before the Enzo's launch to existing customers who had bought F40s and F50s), but then, rather brilliantly, they offered to make one final car for the Pope, John Paul II. His Holiness eventually auctioned that Enzo, raising £720,000 ($1.2 million) for charity. (And who says supercars can't be good for the community?!)

BELOW ***The Maserati MC12 was a race-style supercar mechanically derived from the Enzo (sharing its engine, gearbox and chassis), as Maserati was owned by Ferrari at the time. The car was developed for racing in the FIA GT championships, with just 50 road versions made. The MC12 is great-looking and brutally fast, but very wide – in fact, wider than some buses!***

The car is actually called The Enzo Ferrari, not a Ferrari Enzo. At the time of launch, Ferrari called the Enzo 'the pinnacle of our technological achievement'. Was the Enzo the greatest Ferrari ever built? Probably not, but it seems certain that the marque's racing-obsessed founder would have been thrilled with this F1 car for the road.

2002 Koenigsegg CC8S

The supercar world is famous for new players entering the market with a big fanfare of ambition and promise before, two or three years later and often saddled with huge debts and failed dreams, this new-marque-on-the-block ignominiously goes bankrupt. The costs of developing a supercar are now so great that this is an inevitable consequence of the 'survival of the fittest/fastest' race among manufacturers. Some put the figure of developing a new supercar from scratch at £750 million ($1.26 billion). A high-tech steering wheel with LED functionality alone can cost £10 million ($17 million).

This is not so, however, for Swedish upstart Koenigsegg. This brilliant manufacturer came to the supercar party in 2002, and the sheer brute force of its cars combined with stunning looks and the exquisite detail of its finished product has made this a very serious supercar contender indeed. The man behind the badge is Christian von Koenigsegg, who was inspired

BELOW ***An extreme evolution of the Enzo came with the Ferrari FXX. At a price of £1.1 million ($1.8 million), it was the most expensive supercar ever built at the time. Boasting a highly tuned 800bhp engine, these 29 Ferraris really were F1 cars for the road. The FXX was not street legal and was garaged by Ferrari, who maintained it ready for track use only.***

to build his own supercar by a Norwegian stop-motion film about a bicycle repair man who builds a racing car, which Christian watched when he was just five years old. As a child, he dismantled toasters and video recorders, and by his teens he was sought after locally for his prowess at tuning mopeds. Then, in 1994, at the age of just 22, he set up his own supercar company, despite having no mainstream automotive experience (he had, instead, been very successful with a food exporting company). Christian's ambition was simple: to create the perfect supercar.

This ambition was matched by drive, which fired Christian to launch his first production car, the Koenigsegg CC8S, in 2002. However, the car that really set the supercar world alight was the CCX (Competition Coupe X), launched in 2006. This was a twin-supercharged, carbon-fibre-bodied bullet, using a heavily modified, 4.7-litre Ford V8 engine to create a whopping 806bhp and blistering performance. *Top Gear*'s The Stig famously crashed a CCX on the show's test track, after which Koenigsegg offered a rear spoiler.

Each of Koenigsegg's ferocious, mid-engined cars is hand-built, with over 300 carbon-fibre parts used in each car, which take over 1,000 man hours to make. The uncluttered, stunning looks are defined by Koenigsegg's famous forward cabins and long, powerful tails. The company works from a disused jet-fighter base in southern Sweden with its own mile-long runway (Sweden is renowned for its jet-fighter technology). The runway also doubles as a landing spot for customers' private jets and helicopters. The previous facility was damaged in a fire, but Christian and his fellow employees were able to save from the flames some of the crucial car parts and design sketches.

Koenigsegg quickly set out to lead the supercar field in alternative fuels too. The CCXR was a very low-volume biofuel roadster released in 2008. This was no 'hippy' ecologist's car, though, offering 1018bhp and a 245mph top speed, even though it can run on bioethanol as well as standard petrol.

ABOVE **The flying ghost insignia of the Swedish Air Force's Fighter Jet Squadron No.1 adorns the glass engine cover of every Koenigsegg, in deference to their production facilities' previous owner. Koenigsegg's own company badge is based on the family coat of arms, which has existed since the 12th century.**

SUPERCAR FACT
There are plans to make a three-car run based on the CCX, called the Trevita, which will be made from a special diamond-coated carbon fibre. This will retain the marque's distinctive scissor doors, whose opening action is called 'dihedral syncro-helix actuation', that are unique to Koenigsegg.

Koenigsegg claims to have run a CCXR to 260mph in private testing, although even that speed has since been usurped by the company's latest evolution. The Agera (meaning 'to take action' in Swedish) is an even more ballistic machine: an all-carbon, twin-turbo, V8, rear-driven car with no traction control. The 'basic' model produces 940bhp, though there is an 'R' derivative offering a staggering 1,115bhp. This extreme power is matched by incredible lightness, with even the drive shafts made hollow to save weight. The Agera can also run on biofuel and has a theoretical top speed of a world-beating 275mph. One proven world record held by the Agera is for the time taken to go from 0 to 300km/h and back to 0km/h – a staggering 21.9 seconds.

Amazingly, for all this, the Agera can still be fitted with a roofbox for customers' skis. At night, some of the interior controls are illuminated by microfibres (carbon nanotubes) implanted into the aluminium surfaces. Amazingly, the Agera has a reasonably large boot and luxurious interior, with full-leather furnishings, CD player and options such as GPS, rear-view camera, a phone system as well as bespoke suitcases.

In March 2014, the firm unveiled the so-called One:1; an ultra-light version of the Agera, producing 1,360bhp, giving it a 1:1 power to weight ratio, weighing, as it does, 1,360kg. This power output is the equivalent of one megawatt, which, Koenigsegg claims, makes the One:1 the world's first 'megacar'. The top speed of 273mph, if verified, would make the One:1 a Veyron-beating world-record holder.

Every Koenigsegg offers a raw, pure-driving experience: hugely loud and devastatingly rapid. You have to admire Christian's sheer determination as well as the purity of his vision. Along with Pagani, Koenigsegg has established itself as a genuine new supercar marque for the new millennium.

BELOW **One Koenigsegg owner was said to have been given the 'fastest' speeding ticket in the world, having allegedly been clocked at 242mph.**

GAME CHANGER

2005 Bugatti Veyron

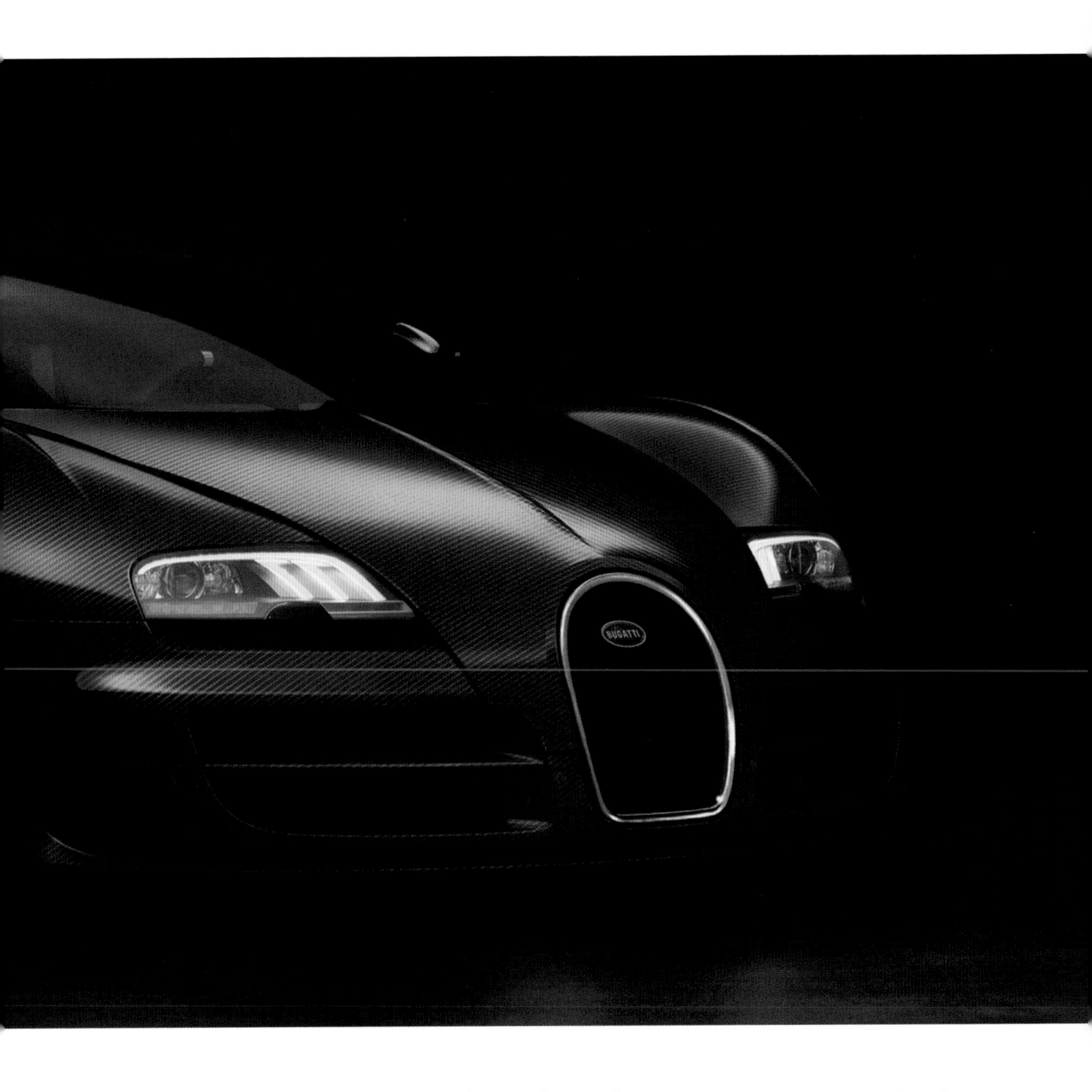

I HAVE TO DECLARE A SPECIAL INTEREST in my ninth game changer, the Bugatti Veyron, or Beast from the East (of France), as it is known. In 2011, I wrote a book called *Bugatti Veyron: A Quest for Perfection, The Story of the Greatest Car in the World* (available online and from all good book stores, I might add!). So, I have nailed my colours to the mast in one sense. However, the reason I wrote that book is also an indication of just why this frankly breathtaking machine – the world's fastest production car – carries such caché...

I was in London, enjoying a weekend with my family. It was mid-afternoon, and we were driving through Mayfair on a quest to spot nice cars

ABOVE ***The Bugatti Veyron Super Sport: the fastest production car in the world.***

cars (my wife was thrilled). As we turned one particularly expensive corner of this über-rich ghetto, there, on the left, parked up and with the roof off, was a Veyron Grand Sport, the convertible, £1.5 million ($2.05 million). The car was white, the number plate was just two digits and the driver had pulled over to make a phone call, it seemed. My heart rate leaped up, and so I swerved my car into a parking space so expensive, you needed a credit card to pay the fee, but I didn't care. My physical reaction on seeing my first Veyron was so visceral that I had to get out and take a proper look. I bundled my two little petrol-heads out of the car and walked up alongside the Bugatti. My breathing had become shallow, and I was genuinely as excited as my two lads. I nodded politely to the man in the car, gesturing for his permission to take a photo. He nodded and smiled. As I snapped away, I couldn't help but notice the watch on his arm: definitely worth more than my car, maybe more than my house.

I took the photo and headed back to my car. As I buckled up, I realised that I had reacted to the Veyron in *exactly* the same way as when I see a famous celebrity. It is a physical reaction: a rush of adrenaline, a surge of excitement. I am lucky enough that my trade is as a ghostwriter, so I deal with celebrities quite often, but there are still some famous faces that leave you – to use the cliché – starstruck. The Veyron was just such a celebrity. So, I wondered, if the car was a celebrity, why didn't I 'ghostwrite' its story?

So I did.

I ghostwrote for the fastest car in the world. I interviewed everyone who had been pivotal to the Veyron's creation: Bugatti's president, the chief engineer of the car, its test driver and top-speed world record-holder ('pilot', as his card described), its super-intelligent brand historian, as well as some customers. I travelled across Europe, to the pristine assembly laboratory where they construct this car – entirely by hand over a period of weeks and weeks – in the Alsace region of northeast France, next to an old chateau once owned by the brand's founder, Ettore Bugatti. Bugatti came from a family of artists, and his creations, such as the Royale and Atlantic, are more art than engineering.

I also travelled to Germany, to 'Car City', the Autostadt that the VW Group called its home. Then – and yes, I still pinch myself that this actually

LEFT **The Bugatti Atlantic is the most expensive car of all time, with a recent example selling for a rumoured £24 million ($40 million) plus.**

happened – I did 201mph in a Bugatti Veyron Super Sport on the autobahn. Better still, I had as my co-driver that day Dr Wolfgang Schreiber, the chief engineer of the Veyron, a capaciously brilliant man who is one of the most important automotive minds of the modern era (more from him later).

So, enough about my book, but what about the celebrity at the heart of its story? *Why* is the Bugatti Veyron such a headturner? Let's start with just the bare statistics: an 8-litre engine in a so-called W16 configuration to create an engine capable of an apocalyptic 1,001bhp. Then they strapped on four turbos. Then they added ten radiators. Then they inserted a dual-clutch gearbox capable of changing gear in 150 milliseconds. A top speed of 253mph – a world record – soon followed. And all of this was packaged in a car that – to cite Bugatti's own criterion when they were developing the £1.5 billion ($2.5 billion) project – you could drive easily to the opera.

ABOVE ***The Vitesse – the fastest open-top car ever built.***

BUGATTI

ABOVE ***A collection of Bugattis at the Jack Barclay dealership in Mayfair, London, England.***

Complete with air-conditioning, luxurious seats, a sound system, rear-view camera, parking sensors and all the other mod cons you could want in a 21st-century car.

The story of the Veyron is a long and complicated one (someone should write a book about it): Dr Ferdinand Piech, the grandson of Ferry Porsche, had long admired the brutal power of the Porsche 917 that cleaned up at Le Mans in 1970/1. Piech became fascinated with the notion of putting 1,001bhp in a road car. He actually wrote his criteria for the Veyron on a napkin: 1,001bhp; 0–60mph in less than 3 seconds; a top speed in excess of 250mph; and, yes, you would need to be able to drive it to the opera.

Many years of difficulties and delayed launches followed, before my test drive companion Dr Wolfgang Schreiber and his team finally launched the Veyron in 2005. Like the McLaren F1 before it, the Veyron completely and utterly redefined the notion of a supercar overnight. The brand had somehow achieved the three statistical criteria for the car, and in so doing created the fastest production car the world had ever seen. From my own experience, I can confirm the last criterion – being able to drive it to the opera – was also achieved. (I actually went to a service station rather than the opera, but you get the point.)

The car has a very feminine silhouette and hunkers down, drawing itself on to the tarmac. Its curvaceous form is also deceptive, because this two-tonne vehicle is actually rather petite in the flesh. When at high speed, the rear wing can alter its angle in split-seconds, thanks to laser technology taken from the aerospace industry. That same rear wing creates as much downforce on its own as a small family car.

This added braking power is a good thing, because in a Veyron you might find you need to stop rather suddenly from *very* high speeds. When I was driving the Super Sport, I found myself 'tootling along' and chatting at around 150mph, initially unaware of the speed because the car was barely using a quarter of its horses and the engine was almost silent. Then, I noticed a contraflow up ahead going into one lane, which I was approaching at about 135mph (while merrily talking about Bayern Munich). I avoided disaster and, so, I can verify that the Veyron brakes are very, *very* good.

You will need some pretty impressive figures of your own to buy a Veyron. The 'entry level' model – the Dacia Duster, if you will – was £810,345 ($1,366,533) on launch day. The orange and black liveried 1,200bhp Super Sport World Record Edition that I was lucky enough to drive is one of only five, with each now worth around £2.5 million ($4.2 million). The tyres will cost you around £18,000 for a set and are handmade just for the Veyron. New alloys will be approximately £50,000. Should you get in the ridiculously luxurious cabin a little too roughly and happen to snap a magnesium indicator stalk, that will cost you £4,500 to replace. Servicing costs around £11,000. Crunch the bumper and it will set you back around £23,000. New gearbox? That will be £80,000 (although they have never yet had to replace one. Or a clutch. Or an engine. This machine is backed by VW, remember).

The Veyron trumped its competitors by such a margin that it actually appeared to effect a change in strategy for some manufacturers. Ferrari

ABOVE In 2010, the Super Sport edition of the Veyron hit 267.856mph, making it the fastest car in the world. Only five examples of this orange and black edition exist.

were rumoured to have given up the battle for top speed, dismissing it as an irrelevance. In the aftermath of the Veyron, it was noticeable how many top-of-the-line supercars were launched with top speeds just over 200mph, not even trying to get near the 267.856mph of the Super Sport Bugatti. (At that speed, you are travelling the length of a football pitch each time you flick your eyes down to look at the speedometer!)

The Veyron changed the game by being so comprehensively faster and more powerful than any car on the planet and by being so brilliantly engineered. Its performance statistics devastated anything else that called itself a supercar. That Bugatti could achieve this, combined with an ultra level of luxury and supreme ease of use, makes the Veyron a watershed moment in supercar history.

If you are not lucky enough to ever drive this engineering masterpiece, here's the best way to imagine what it is like when you downshift two gears and then floor the Veyron in a straight line. It is exactly like the moment in *Star Wars* when Han Solo takes the Millennium Falcon to hyperspeed and all those white bolts of stars blur forwards onscreen. When I topped 200mph on that sunny but cold day in Wolfsburg, Germany, the world became a very odd place. My vision was tunnelled, the edges of my sight no more than a blurred haze. The survival instincts of my amateur driver's brain let me process only what was needed in order to keep me alive – namely, the road directly in front of me. Maybe it was the relative stress of the situation, but I don't remember there being any noise – perhaps, as I say, because my brain was ignoring any senses that weren't essential. So, if you think about that, what this means is that with the all-conquering Veyron, Bugatti created a car that was almost too powerful for the human brain to fully compute. At the time of writing, the Veyron is the undisputed king of the supercar world and has been for almost a decade.

Bugatti Veyron

LAUNCHED

2005

POWER

The bhp is 1,001 in the standard car Veyron 16.4 and the Grand Sport roadster and 1,200 bhp in the Super Sport and Grand Sport Vitesse roadster

ACCELERATION

The Super Sport edition is capable of 0–60mph in 2.4 secs

MAXIMUM SPEED

The Super Sport edition reached a world record speed of 267.856mph

PRODUCTION RUN

Bugatti made 300 coupes and are scheduled to make 150 convertibles

LEFT ***The cabin of a Veyron 'Nocturne' edition – one of a number of very limited-edition versions of this ultimate supercar.***

RIGHT ***The Veyron needs ten radiators to keep the massive engine cool, while the engine bay itself is uncovered.***

GRAND SPORT

2009 Aston Martin One-77

Aston Martin repeatedly wins the 'Coolest Brand in the World' award – not just for car brands but for *any* brand. This extraordinary manufacturer has made some sumptuous cars over the decades, of course – the DB4, DB5, AMV600 Vantage, various Vanquish models, etc. – but there is one car that undoubtedly has to be included in any book of pivotal supercars: the One-77.

As the name suggests, this vehicle was strictly limited to a run of just 77 cars, with each selling for a massive £1,150,000 ($1.9 million). Astons are not the cheapest cars, of course, but with tax added, this was almost ten times the price of some of their other models. The hype surrounding the car had been building ever since its first, brief appearance at the Paris Motor Show in 2008. Aston said the car's rapid development time – just four years – had two clear objectives: first, to build the fastest, most radical and most advanced Aston ever made, and, second, to create a model that would filter down into future Astons. Following a few pre-launch leaks and a couple of sneak previews of only some parts of the car, the One-77 was formally revealed at the Geneva Motor Show in 2009. And what a stunner it was.

The car has a 7.3-litre, V12 front engine creating 750bhp through the rear wheels, the most powerful normally aspirated engine ever made. Anyone who has been in the car will testify that the noise of this engine is staggering. A high-tech approach also saw 'Dynamic Suspension Spool Valves' used, a world first for a road car (which would be great if I actually knew what they did!). Jokes aside, each car's suspension was individually set up by Aston engineers to suit each customer's preference. And the personalisation service did not stop there, with customers able to choose bespoke gearbox settings, interior trim, seats, pedals and more. The One-77 also had a full carbon-fibre monocoque chassis weighing just 180kg.

The long, bumperless, nosed body was classic Aston Martin yet also extremely futuristic-looking, with aggressive strakes behind the front wheel, creases on the doors, distinctive tail lights and a massive rear diffuser. The stunning body panels were handmade in aluminium. The amazing, sweeping front wings are each made from a single piece of aluminium, by hand, taking one person three weeks per wing. Each panel was bonded to the chassis using a process created for Airbus aeroplanes. Huge, flared rear wheel arches give the One-77 a very aggressive stance (wider than a Veyron), and this is exaggerated still further by the adaptive rear spoiler that pops up at high speed. And you will need that high-speed balance because the quoted top speed of 200mph was smashed in official tests, reaching 220mph. Just as well, then, that carbon-ceramic brakes came as standard.

The so-called 'butterfly' doors – a variant of the supercar scissor door – slid open to offer up a sumptuous cabin. The same doors were fully skinned inside with bare carbon, as were the door sills, floor and bulkhead; the rest of the interior was a mixture of more carbon, high-grade leather, anodised aluminium and rose gold. Starting the car involves a key that appears to have a crystal on the end. Aston themselves called the car 'a piece of automotive art'.

ABOVE ***The Aston Martin One-77 is ridiculously quick: 0–60mph in 3.7 seconds and reportedly almost a full second quicker to 100mph than a Koenigsegg CCX.***

There were a few complaints about the gearbox, but overall the car was met with rabidly positive reviews. And it wasn't just the press who fell in love with this amazing supercar – wealthy car collectors did, too, with all 77 examples selling out very quickly (this, despite the car being launched during a severe global financial crisis).

The One-77 won numerous design awards even before it was launched, and the car has set a new bar for Aston Martin, already one of the greatest car brands of all time. Make no mistake: the One-77 can be quite vicious. It is a deceptively brutish supercar, despite the still-elegant silhouette – the words 'malevolent' and 'savage' were often used in reviews. In an Aston Martin – a marque better known for a very English kind of motoring refinement – this can only be a good thing. If the One-77 sets a template for forthcoming Aston Martins, then the future is very exciting indeed.

2010 Lexus LFA

As I have already mentioned, with reference to two remarkable exceptions to the rule – Pagani and Koenigsegg – it is unusual for a newcomer to enter the supercar market and truly ruffle feathers. It is yet more unusual that any true contender should come from outside the established geographical parameters. The Honda NSX, as we have seen, was a brilliant new 'outsider' addition, but in 2010, Lexus, a company better known for its refined and, let's be frank, slightly dull executive cars, produced a supercar that was, literally, in a different class: the LFA. This was, as Lexus said, a supercar with 'a Samurai spirit'.

The car began as a secretive project, codenamed P280, first revealed as a dramatic, glass-roofed, triple-exhaust concept car at a well-received unveiling in 2005. However, it was a full ten years before the car reached production, by which time critics were getting restless and technology had moved on considerably. Nonetheless, when the LFA arrived, it was a great-

looking car, as much like a hot hatch in the style of *Fast and Furious* as a supercar, but very definitely with the performance of the latter.

Lexus's parent company Toyota had been keen to make the most of the technology used in its F1 cars, and the LFA was the perfect foil for that. Carbon-fibre-reinforced polymers were used for the monocoque tub, plus paddle shift gears and a layout that created almost perfect balance front to rear (48%/52%).

The 65% carbon-fibre LFA had a 552bhp, 4.8-litre V10 engine – developed with Yamaha motorbike technology – that could rev to 10,000rpm in less than a second. (Lexus found that a physical rev needle couldn't actually keep up, so they had to use a digital display instead.) Yet, somehow, Lexus made the engine so compact as to be smaller than most V8s. It is the noise of this engine that is universally regarded as the LFA's high point, with every reviewer commenting on how exactly like an F1 car it was: evidence of the extensive acoustic manipulation, done in collaboration with musical instrument manufacturers during development. Toyota engineers actually tune the vibrations and sounds from the engine, which are then funnelled into the cabin at foot and ear level. They called this noise 'the roar of an angel': a roar that would later be heard across race tracks around the world, as the LFA enjoyed a very successful racing career.

LEFT ***Despite its lengthy gestation, the Lexus LFA made a massive impact on its launch and is widely regarded as a very accomplished supercar.***

The statistics were impressive, too: 0–60mph in 3.7 seconds and a top speed of 202mph. The interior dashboard was more like a games console extravaganza than a car. The motor trade was hugely impressed, with the LFA receiving widespread rave reviews. The car has now started to filter down its technology into Toyota's and Lexus's wider ranges. Only 500 cars were made, each at an astonishing price of £340,000 ($575,000), yet every single one sold before production even began. If you didn't have the money to buy an actual LFA, there was an online configurator offering over 30 billion digital combinations of the car.

The Lexus LFA is an unlikely supercar, but one whose performance, technology, critical reception, motor racing success and sheer ambition deserves full recognition.

2011 Lamborghini Aventador

With supercars evolving into ever-more complex animals, there are some people who bemoan the loss of a so-called 'analogue' supercar, where driver aids do not get in the way of the pure driving experience. Supporters of this school of thought would swap an Enzo Ferrari for a Ferrari F40 every time, or maybe they'd buy the Noble M600 (more of which later) instead of a Ferrari 458. It is old-school versus new-school.

Yet supercars do need to evolve, they need to pioneer, and it is not feasible to stubbornly make analogue cars for the sake of it. The new generation of supercar customers will want to see progress. This is where the Lamborghini Aventador comes in because, in my opinion, it is the best supercar in the world at offering a combination of old-school thrills and new-era technology.

ABOVE ***The press release for the Lamborghini Aventador said, 'Design is always the beauty of aggressive power, the elegance of breathtaking dynamics.' Innit.***

The Festival of Speed is perhaps as good a place as any to unveil a new supercar: rolling green acres of fast dream machines, classic cars, stalls and events mixing with the smell of burning rubber and a waft of fried onions and hot dogs. A heaven on earth for the petrol-head. Nestled down near the West Sussex coast, it is a quintessentially British event, being the home of the Duke of Richmond and set in the grounds of the spectacular Goodwood House.

At the 2011 event, in a discreet corner of this vast site (yet just a few hundred yards away from the start of the Festival's famous hillclimb race) was a pristine white marquee hidden away from the masses. Outside the immaculate awning stood two large security guards clad in beautiful suits, alongside two tall and elegantly manicured hostesses. I was greeted with a glass of cold champagne and a silver plate of canapés, before being invited inside. After the bright West Sussex sunshine, my eyes momentarily had to adjust to the dimmer light inside and when they did, they quickly began to focus on the beast that lay in wait. And it was a beast: the Lamborghini Aventador.

This car was launched in early 2011, following huge anticipation among the supercar world. This was post-Veyron, and with other supercar players such as Pagani and Koenigsegg now firmly established in the marketplace, all eyes were on what Lamborghini would do next. Did the famously extravagant, bold supercar marque still have what it took?

Easy answer: yes.

Even standing 20 feet away from the Aventador, I instantly realised this was a classic new Lamborghini. The greatest car they had made since the Audi takeover, certainly, but maybe their greatest car ever. I'm not alone in that assumption, as the car was widely hailed as a modern classic on its launch. *Evo* magazine said there was 'little doubt that the Aventador is the best V12 Lamborghini have ever made.'

So, why is the Aventador so good?

In many ways, it is a very conventional supercar, or at least a conventional Lamborghini: V12, very wide, very powerful and very low. It has stunning looks, displayed best of all in the various loud colours that Lamborghinis are so famous for. The car publicly launched a design theme that had been partly showcased in the Batman-esque Reventon concept car and to a lesser degree the more sedate Estoque concept. The car was styled entirely on computer and maximised a central theme of hexagons, with over 200 used on the entire vehicle.

However, this car was much more than just aesthetics; this was genuine automotive blood and thunder. As with all modern Lamborghinis, the Aventador was named after a famous fighting bull; in this case, the Aventador's namesake was renowned in the early 1990s for its spirit and courage in battle. A fitting moniker then for the hell and fury that lay underneath the engine covers. In a sense, that same courage can be attributed to the marque for having the nerve to launch a large, bold, V12 supercar in an era when the watchwords are hybrid technology and carbon footprints.

The Aventador can sprint to 60mph in less than 3 seconds (2.9, to be precise) and onwards to a top speed of 217mph. This is made possible by a brand-new, 700bhp, 6.5-litre engine (known internally as the L539), created in-house by Lamborghini. Although the brand is renowned for V12s, this was in fact only the second time they had made a V12 themselves, following the beautiful 350GT from the early 1960s. This seismic power is coupled with the use of lightweight materials. This means the carbon-fibre chassis on this big car weighs just 147.5kg, which is the same as a rather large man (who couldn't fit into an Aventador).

The power generated is apocalyptic. At 5,000rpm, the engine starts to come alive, which is ironic because after that, unless you are a very skilful driver indeed, being alive might be exactly the last thing you will actually be doing.

All this power is transferred to the road via an all-wheel drive system, something of a modern Lamborghini speciality – a system helped hugely by the company's association with Audi. The deployable rear spoiler that has become a key feature of so many ultra-modern supercars was also vital in keeping this thing on the ground. For some critics, all this focus on grip was just as well because there was some criticism of the gear change, which *Evo* magazine said when used in 'Corsa' mode was akin to the violence of a train crash. Lamborghini had chosen to buck the trend of double-clutch supercars by using a single-clutch system. Even so, the shift time is a ludicrous 50 milliseconds, which is only a third of the Veyron's lightning-quick gear change.

The Aventador was an entirely new platform, designed to replace the Murcielago, which was itself a successor to the Diablo. The Aventador would certainly change your bank account, too. Spec it up to a decent standard and you can easily spend £295,000 ($500,000). Want the carbon-fibre engine cover? That'll cost £5,000 ($8,400). Add electric heated seats and a rear parking camera and you will add more than a budget family car.

A month after the Festival of Speed, I found myself being offered a drive in the car from Lamborghini's London dealership. I didn't need to be asked twice. I negotiated the spectacular scissor doors and slid quite easily into the cockpit. All mid-engine Lamborghinis of the last 40 years have had iconic scissor doors that make entering the car a spectacle, for both the driver and anyone watching! Once inside, instead of a traditional instrument cluster, the Aventador uses a TFT screen littered with all manner of complex information.

You've paid around £300,000 ($500,000) and have one of the most technologically advanced cars ever built, and yet one of the most exhilarating thrills when you drive an Aventador is flipping up the Top Gun flap that sits over the Start/Stop button and pressing the machine into life. A cheap thrill. Although not that cheap...

First impressions were that it is a big car, only six inches narrower than a double-decker bus, in fact. This was in my mind as I gingerly pulled the Aventador out on to the Westway, London's A40 trunk road that feeds the world into the west side of the capital. The speed limit is 40mph on that fabled road, which seemed almost impossible to do in the Aventador without actually taking my foot off the accelerator altogether. Yet, surprisingly, the car was nimble; once I was accustomed to the size and ferocious power sitting right behind my head, it was a refined and easy drive. The suspension has been criticised, too, but any shortcomings here were not apparent on my urban test drive.

The gear change was indeed very distinct, but I couldn't help thinking that if a Veyron can change gear in the time it takes to blink your eye, and the Aventador is even quicker, to a degree we had reached the point where gear changes were probably fast enough for most mere mortals.

BELOW ***Stephan Winkelmann, Lamborghini's chairman, confidently called the Roadster convertible version of the Aventador 'the most extraordinary Lamborghini in the company's illustrious 50-year history.' That subverts the conventional wisdom that convertible cars are never as good at handling or performance as their coupe counterparts. The Roadster shares the coupe's top speed of 217mph. Just imagine that with the roof down!***

This is a thoroughly 21st century-Lamborghini. There are even nods to the eco-fanatics with a stop-start system, an ultra-efficient recharging process for the battery and the ability to use fewer cylinders at lower speeds for better fuel consumption. Luggage space is modest on the coupe and almost non-existent when the roof of the convertible is stowed away, but Lamborghini pragmatically state that 'you don't buy a car like this to go shopping with.'

One critic called this the 'friendliest V12 supercar ever'. Yet somehow that wasn't allowed to dilute the brutality that the brand is famous for. If you want to drive the Aventador at full pelt, you will need to have a very long straight and/or the mind of a certified maniac.

This ease of use was a huge relief to me, as I nervously guided this £300,000 ($500,000) car around London's busy streets, but in fact it is also a far more important statement. In that sense, it is indicative of a new generation of Lamborghinis, of which the Aventador is the most high-profile example. Gone are the days when you had to have arm muscles like Popeye to steer a Lamborghini around a corner, or when you needed a lottery win to replace the clutch that you would burn unless you made a perfect hill start. Corner in the wet at more than 10mph and you might as well phone the tow truck on the way round as you approach the ditch. You expect any rear visibility? How very dare you!

BELOW ***The Lamborghini Huracán: the replacement for the commercially successful Gallardo and a direct descendant of the more brutish Aventador.***

Not so with the Aventador. This is why this car is a game changer, for Lamborghini at least. Because when Lamborghini get it right, *everyone* sits up and takes notice. The boys buying the posters for their bedroom walls notice, the aspiring supercar buyers notice, the supercar collectors notice, and the designers and engineers at every other supercar company the world over take heed, too. Lamborghini has a very particular brand image, and yes, it's not for everybody, but with the Aventador, a new generation of Lamborghinis was announced to the world. And the world had to listen. Not least because what else sounds like *that*!

What the Aventador also did for Lamborghini was re-inject a little – well, frankly – a little madness back into the brand. The Aventador seemed to create quite a buzz on the internet, too – check out the man on Youtube trying to cook a Christmas turkey with the 2-foot flames from the car's exhaust, complete with the car dressed up as Rudolf the Red Nosed Reindeer. Now *that* is a supercar.

There is even a 1:8 scale model version, wrapped in gold by designer Robert Gülpen, which was on sale for 18 times the price of an actual car, in the region of £4.5 million ($7.5 million). It is mounted behind a bullet-proof case, with a logo made of gold, platinum and gemstones. Should anyone try to steal your gold model, then the Dubai police force actually has an Aventador in its fleet of cop cars.

Then there was perhaps the most striking of all the limited-edition cars, the Sesto Elemento (albeit based on the so-called 'Baby Lambo', the Gallardo, itself a stunning supercar), a Batmobile for the post-credit crunch generation, topping out at the £2 million ($3.4 million) mark. What credit crunch…

ABOVE ***In the wake of the Aventador, Lamborghini released a number of stunning concept cars and also limited-edition vehicles. The Aventador J was a roofless, windowless cartoon bullet on wheels. The three-car run Veneno – meaning venom – was based on the Aventador, launched to celebrate the brand's fiftieth anniversary and costing an eye-watering £1.85 million ($3.12 million). All sold before they were even launched. One interesting gadget was the G Meter, which displayed the G-forces being experienced under hard cornering, although quite how safe it is to be looking at a display on the dashboard when you are generating G-forces from sheer cornering speed is not clear. The Veneno Roadster was launched on an aircraft carrier in Abu Dhabi.***

Despite this intense interest in the car, Lamborghini are not about to make the Aventador a high-volume model. The car is reported to be limited to just 4,000 units, partly verified by the fact that the moulds for the carbon-fibre monocoque only last for 500 cars each, with only eight reported to be in existence.

Fast-forward three years and I am standing in an industrial former meat-packing factory in the East End of London. Also in the room are an elite selection of customers, all eyeing curiously the silk-curtained corner of the room, where we know the new Lamborghini Huracán is sitting, waiting for its UK launch. There is perhaps as much pressure on this car to succeed as there had been on the Aventador back at Goodwood. This will be a higher-volume seller, more affordable – relatively, as it is still in excess of £200,000 ($340,000) with a high spec – and hopefully the torch-bearer for the brand heading into the future.

The presentation tells me that this car has 'instinctive technology', achieves nearly 90% of torque at just 1,000rpm and has whippet-fast velocity. It is crafted with the same hexagonal obsession as the Aventador, even down to the *Top Gun*-style switches inside for the windows and air conditioning.

In one corner of the room I spot a Lamborghini salesman taking an order less than five minutes after the curtain had been pulled away. I ask him, if I wanted to buy one, when I would be able to take delivery. 'They're already pre-sold for about two years.'

Only time will tell if this beautiful car will replicate the landmark impact of the Aventador, but suffice to say, if this is the way that Lamborghini are heading, then the watershed Aventador will just be the first of many stellar new super sports cars from this most extravagant of supercar brands. Lamborghini describe themselves as 'uncompromising, extreme, Italian', and this car is certainly all of the above. The Aventador represents a spectacular return to form.

2012 Pagani Huayra

Named after an Andean god of wind, the Huayra was an object of obsession for its mercurial creator. Pagani was painstaking in his approach to the car's development, not signing it off until every last tiny detail was perfected (it was tested over more than one million miles). Longer and wider than the Zonda, it carries a custom-made, 7-litre, twin-turbo, 730bhp, AMG V12 engine. It is made chiefly from carbotanium – carbon fibre laced with titanium threads that have been soaked in a resin whose recipe is known only by Horacio Pagani. The monocoque is designed to shear off in the event of a sideways impact, deliberately separating from the car to divert the energy from the collision away from the cabin. The Huayra has active aerodynamics on the front and rear of the car and four independent panels, which automatically rise and fall depending on whether the car needs either downforce or less drag. The interior, as with the Zonda, looks like a jewellery store window. Its shape was inspired by the wing of an aircraft, and with its gullwing doors and stunning silhouette, the Huayra looks ready for take-off.

2015 Bentley Continental GT Speed

The Bentley Continental is not a conventional supercar: it is not a vehicle that altered the way supercars were designed the day after its launch. However, what it did do *for me* was shock me with its stunning combination of performance and luxury. I was lucky enough to be given a test car for a weekend that coincided with a dear family friend being very ill over five hours' drive away. It was potentially a very long and very stressful journey. This car was so complete, so comfortable and so beautifully engineered that it was like being picked up and carefully placed at our destination point in moments. 'That's a GT, then.' I hear you say. That's okay; that's your opinion. On paper I can agree. It even has that term in its name. But, to me, this car is a very modern representation of supercars. A very personal choice.

Supercars are generally seen as a rather modern phenomenon, at least in terms of the cartoonish road bullets that make up much of this book. However, as I mentioned earlier, there is a vast prehistory – prior to the likes of the Mercedes-Benz Gullwing, the Miura and the 911 – of manufacturers creating absolutely outrageous cars, lightning quick for their time, crammed with innovative engineering. Cars that truly pushed out the boundaries.

Case in point: the Bentley Blower.

So almost four decades before my 'modern' supercars even came into existence, Bentley were making ludicrously fast cars. It was with this in mind

BELOW ***The Zonda's successor, the Huayra, named after an Andean god of wind, has unique wing mirrors set on curved, elongated stalks, designed to look like a beautiful woman's eye.***

that I caught the train to the Bentley factory, situated in Crewe, a railway town in the northwest of England, where the car maker is the main employer. I was in search of the Continental GT Speed, the fastest and most-powerful Bentley ever.

On arrival at the factory, you are greeted by an immaculate glass reception and a wall of televisions showing new Bentley models scything through country roads. This glossy welcome is situated adjacent to the huge factory, which employs around 3,700 people. Just behind the reception desk is the start of a Bentley factory tour that in two hours perfectly displays why this brand is such a unique and necessary addition to this book.

I was met for my tour by a crisply besuited man who proudly told me he had worked for Bentley since he was sweeping up the factory floor aged just 17. He proceeded to show me the history of the marque, which only reinforced just how unique it is. He spoke of W.O. Bentley, an English gentleman who founded the company way back in 1919, in Cricklewood, and how the very early models started winning races almost immediately. He told me how the brand quickly began to appeal to a generation of 'gentleman racers' who, along with the likes of Ettore Bugatti and Enzo Ferrari, populated the racing circuits of the era. I learned of Bentley's multiple Le Mans victories (five in the first decade), which started just four years after the first production car had been built. Bentley were also the first company to use aluminium pistons, rather than the standard of cast iron. It seems innovation was always key.

Further, I heard about the so-called Bentley Boys: a famous group of rich men who are inexorably associated with the brand and who came to typify the lifestyle of excess, extremes and risk that would define the marque's early years. This group of wealthy men from the upper classes raced hard and played hard. Among their lavish ranks were an aviator, a pearl fisherman, a diamond magnate, a steeplechaser and various financiers whose antics on and off the race track kept the company's profile high. On one occasion, the prominent Bentley Boy Woolf 'Babe' Barnato was at a party in Cannes, France and boldly claimed that he could get to London in his Bentley Speed Six faster than the Blue Train Express could get to Calais, with enough time left over to be sitting with a drink in hand in his London club. The gauntlet was thrown down, a £100 ($160) bet was placed, a race was made and Babe did exactly that. He won by four minutes.

When Bentley hit financial difficulties in the Great Depression era of the late 1920s and 1930s, members of the Bentley Boys bought the company and this era witnessed the aforementioned Bentley Blower. Over the coming decades, there would be a number of chequered patches in the Bentley story, switching between making beautiful, luxurious models to almost going out of business, being bought by Rolls Royce, then ending up in many people's eyes as being almost indistinguishable from that luxury brand. Decades before, Ettore Bugatti had called Bentleys 'the world's fastest lorries', and as the 1980s turned, it seemed the world might have fallen out of love with this distinctive British marque. By the early 1980s, there was a real danger of the marque becoming extinct but, following a resurgence with the Continental R as well as the premium Mulsanne models, the situation improved until, in 1997, the VW Group bought the marque in its entirety.

My tour complete, I was by now anxious to see the cars that were the product of this colourful history. As we finally walked into the factory itself, despite the size of the buildings and the high-tech assembly lines rammed with computers and robots, it was hard not to notice the 'boutique' feel of the place. I stopped to chat to the craftsmen and craftswomen – that is the only word for them – who were lovingly wrapping the steering wheels in premium leather. (Bentley's interior leatherwork is perhaps unrivalled.) One chap told me he had been working there since his late teens, as had his father before him. Generations of artisans. This family connection was repeated again and again as I sauntered around the vast space, while semi-constructed Bentleys gradually came to life in front of my eyes. These people were employees, yes, but they all seemed to have one thing in common: they had Bentley in their blood.

BELOW ***Shocking power, surprisingly deft handling and sublime luxury – is the Bentley Continental GT Speed a new breed of supercar?***

LEFT ***Not your usual plastic switch gear: the inside of a Bentley GT Speed.***

RIGHT ***International jet-setter – a Bentley Continental GT Speed outside one of my many international homes. I think this one's in the Bahamas but I lose track. Honest.***

As a brand, Bentley pride themselves on offering a fully bespoke service, where the customer can choose from an almost limitless array of options, colours and materials. One of the most fascinating rooms on the tour allows you to choose your own bespoke elements, including wood, metal, trim and so on.

Just as we approached the end of the tour, I noticed one particular soft-topped Bentley that looked far more aggressive – menacing, even – waiting in a side bay to go through its final meticulous checks. It was a Bentley Continental GT Speed.

The Continental moniker was first introduced on a Bentley way back in 1952. However, it was the relaunch model of 2003 that seemed to propel Bentley back into the spotlight, as the car was instantly favoured by the media as well as a number of high-profile celebrities and sports personalities. The car was an instant hit, and the Crewe factory had to work frantically to keep up with orders.

The 2015 Continental GT Speed is a significant evolution from that original model. The Speed's V12 engine is made up of two banks of six cylinders and twin turbos creating 626bhp that combined constant four-wheel drive and blistering pace with a quiet and luxurious ride. The GT Speed is faster to 60mph than a Porsche 911 Carrera 4S and can push on to 206mph.

The cabin is not so much a car interior as a six-star hotel on wheels. The seats are ultra-comfortable, the polished metal knobs and switches look like they are straight out of a gentlemen's club and the expertly machined gear knob is yet another stand-out detail.

I was apprehensive about taking the car out on the wet roads around Crewe, but the GT Speed's grip is sensational. True to its core personality as a Grand Tourer, the motorways were eaten up with disdain, but I was particularly surprised by the handling, which was incredibly nimble (the majority of power is funnelled by the all-wheel drive system to the rear wheels), and I had to keep reminding myself I was in such a big and heavy car. And despite the hard suspension that provides such tight cornering, the car still had that famous Bentley 'glide' – a seemingly contradictory yet pleasing combination.

Many people will mock the fact that I have included a GT tourer like the Bentley in this supercar book, but in a sense that is the point of its inclusion: to make you rethink your definition of a modern supercar. The GT Speed is a deceptive car. Should you wish to make a quick exit from a standing start, you can be over 3 miles away in less than a minute. Some people might question if it is a supercar at all, because of its touring genesis and ease of use. In my opinion, it is exactly what can be classified as a new generation of supercar – deceptive because it cocoons you in extreme, sublime luxury, but capable of quite staggering performance, too. In my opinion, the GT Speed's performance is genuinely that of a supercar, and it should not be disqualified just because it is luxurious, too. Never forget, stab that throttle down and the GT Speed instantly turns into a beast. This car is Dr Jekyll and Mr Hyde.

Do not be deceived.

SUPERCAR FACT
Rally champion Juha Kankkunen drove a Supersport to a record-breaking 205.48mph in Finland – on ice. Customers can buy the so-called 'ISR' – Ice Speed Record' package.

Also in the 2000s and Onwards

2000 Lotus Exige Although Lotus are one of the greatest sports car manufacturers of all time, this car from the top end of the Elise line is so fast, so peerless with its handling and looks so incredible that it just edges into supercar territory (see also Hennessy Venom GT).

2000 Morgan Aero Established in 1909, Morgan are famous for using wooden (ash) frames on their chassis, beneath an aluminium skin. The Aero was the ultimate high-tech Morgan, perfectly summed up as '21st-century coach-building'. There was just stunning craftsmanship here – no robots or conveyor belts. The Aero is arguably the most unique supercar on the planet.

2001 Aston Martin Vanquish The Vanquish was once described as 'a beast in a silk suit.'

BELOW ***Arguably the sharpest-handling car in the world: the Lotus Exige. A track-day monster.***

ABOVE ***MG SV owner Joe Yapp told me: 'The car is an amazing combination of stunning looks, extensive lightweight carbon-fibre construction and a real V8 grunt. It's a real head turner, and I love taking it out every single time.'***

2001 Lamborghini Murcielago Based on the same platform as the Diablo, the Murcielago had more modernistic looks.

2003 Lamborghini Gallardo The so-called 'Baby Lambo' proved to be a huge commercial success for the marque, selling an incredible 14,000 cars across its ten-year life span. Ferruccio Lamborghini was known to sometimes place a cigarette on the engine block of his cars to make sure they did not vibrate too much; I suspect new owners Audi didn't do that with the Gallardo.

2003 MG SV A hidden gem of the British supercar world, the MG SV was designed by a team led by Peter Stevens – who worked on the McLaren F1. The car used state-of-the-art technology including a lightweight carbon-fibre body, race-inspired chassis, integrated roll-over cage and double wishbone suspension. Elements were made by Italian supercar specialists such as Vaccari and Bosi in Modena, and for that reason, perhaps, the MG SV looks incredible.

ABOVE ***Lamborghini's best-selling 'Baby Lambo', the Gallardo.***

2004 Porsche Carrera GT The Carrera GT was an aggressively stylish but at times tricky-to-handle supercar. With few driver aids, full carbon construction, no turbo and a very low kerb weight (1,380kg), this stunning Porsche had to be driven precisely. A Paris Motor Show concept version was intended only to create a buzz, but was so well liked that Porsche commissioned the car immediately. The 5.7-litre V10 evolved from an F1 engine and a Le Mans block and gives the GT one of the all-time great supercar yowls. (The same yowl your bank account will make when the notorious ceramic clutch goes again.)

2005 Gumpert Apollo The Apollo is, in my opinion, a stunning supercar, although it has been criticised by some for its looks. What can't be criticised, however, is the twin-turbo engine's performance; with a 3.1-second sprint to 60mph and a top speed of 223mph. The company is headed by Roland Gumpert, who was formerly director of sport at Audi during the legendary Audi Quattro rally triumphs. The idea behind Gumpert's cars is to be race-ready but road legal. One of Gumpert's cars has possibly the greatest supercar name ever: the Apollo Enraged!

2006 SC Aero Arguably still yet to fully realise its incredible potential, the super-sleek Aero is a genuine US-bred threat to the Bugatti Veyron in terms of top speed. One to watch!

BELOW ***The Gumpert Apollo's visual signature is an acquired taste, but its performance capability is undeniable.***

ABOVE ***The Caparo T1. Bonkers. Fantastic. I need one.***

2007 Audi R8 The bold new silhouette of the R8 from a previously unknown supercar player was a genuine shock to the establishment. Described as 'the world's most sensible supercar', due to its build quality and reliability, the R8's incredible chassis, all-wheel drive and superb road-holding make this a beast that can also be used for the commute. Despite costing as much as a top Porsche 911, the Audi did gain traction in the supercar world and has since been updated with a brutish V10 version.

2007 Caparo T1 The Caparo is a frankly bonkers race car made legal for the road – and 100% British-built. The car has double the power-to-weight ratio of a Bugatti Veyron and is capable of creating the same cornering G-force as experienced by aerobatic pilots. Just look at it!

2007 Nissan GTR Nissan's GTR is an easily underestimated and certainly understated-looking supercar. Known for blistering performance, the most recent Nismo version is Nissan's fastest-ever car. With a lunatic 591bhp on tap from the 3.8-litre V6, the Nismo's 60mph sprint is claimed to be faster even than a Bugatti Veyron, at 2.4 seconds. The turbochargers are lifted straight from the company's GT3 racers.

2009 Marussia B2 (and B1) The first supercars to come out of Russia, the Marussias offer stunning looks, ballistic performance and limited productions runs – all of which suggest this could be a major new player in the supercar world.

2010 Ferrari 599 GTO A technical masterpiece from Ferrari, the 599 GTO was the fastest Ferrari ever at launch. The car is brimming with technology and made its company so proud that they opted to use the GTO moniker for only the third time in the marque's history (after the legendary 250GTO and 288GTO).

2010 Noble M600 Built in Leicestershire, England, the Noble range of supercars celebrates the driver first and foremost, shunning complex electronic driver aids in favour of a purer experience, akin to cars such as the Ferrari F40. The twin-turbo M600 genuinely rivals the best of the established supercar ranks, with a top speed of 225mph. Having slammed an engine capable of 650bhp into a car that weighs just 1,250kg, the M600 can rocket from 0–60mph in 3.2 seconds – plus 40–60mph takes *one* second. You won't get satellite navigation, climate control, ABS or airbags, but you will get a raw and exhilarating experience like no other. Nick Mason told me that, 'The Noble is brilliant; everyone who drives one loves it. It has a lot of McLaren-esque thinking: a clever simplicity that makes it a real driver's car.' A dark horse in the supercar world, Nobles are rightfully highly prized by many for picking up on a long heritage of 'analogue' supercars that need skilful driving and considered appreciation. Added to that, the Noble is cleverly built to be docile at low speed but a savage tornado at high speed.

BELOW **The Noble M600.**

2010 Ferrari 458 Regarded by many as the most beautiful modern Ferrari of them all, the 458's simply jaw-dropping looks made all supercar manufacturers panic on its launch. But there was substance to the style, with a 563bhp V8 shrieking like a banshee, plus it handled like a top Lotus – astonishingly well. The car's slightly confusing infotainment system does not detract from what is widely regarded as one of the greatest Ferraris ever made.

2011 McLaren MP4-12C The MP4-12C was a searingly fast new supercar from the F1 makers. The 3.8-litre, twin-turbo, V8 engine makes a glorious noise, and, as to be expected from a McLaren, the attention to detail is utterly obsessive. McLaren introduced various elements of active technology, including the ability to brake and/or steer each wheel individually on corners. This is a car that offers astonishingly comfortable ride quality even at low speeds. Around four out of every five 12Cs sold will be the open-topped Spider version. As good at driving around town as it is at ballistic speeds, the 12C faced off against the Ferrari 458 Italia in an almighty supercar battle. Sometimes harshly criticised as too clinical, the 12C is retrospectively winning well-justified plaudits, with subsequent upgrades making the car even more breathtaking. If you want to commute to work in a car that is brutally fast, beautifully engineered and very easy to drive, then the 12C is for you.

BELOW **The McLaren MP4-12C.**

ABOVE ***'Sesto Elemento' translates as 'You won't get this in an underground car park and if you have kids or ever want to go shopping, then buy something else, but if you want to feel like an astronaut in hyperspace every time you accelerate, then this car is for you.' In Italian.***

2011 Lamborghini Sesto Elemento Meaning 'sixth element', as in carbon, the Sesto Elemento is possibly the maddest Lamborghini ever made. At a price of just under £2 million ($3.3 million), the car is made entirely from carbon fibre, with even the prop shaft, suspension and wheel rims forged from carbon. As quick to 60mph as a Bugatti Veyron, the Sesto weighs the same as a Ford Fiesta. This car doesn't look like a Ford Fiesta, though.

2012 Ferrari F12 Berlinetta The fastest Ferrari ever made, the Berlinetta offers 730bhp, a near-three-second sprint to 60mph and a 211mph top speed. What is there not to like?

2012 Hennessy Venom GT Although created from a 'donor' Lotus Exige, rather than being a production car in its own right, the Venom GT has to be considered a leading supercar. The legendary John Hennessy totally rebuilt the car in almost every facet. The Venom's stunning elongated silhouette has top supercar looks, but it is the performance that truly staggers – the Venom missed breaking the Bugatti Veyron Super Sport's world record top speed by a whisker. The theoretical top speed is 274mph, and the Venom already holds the world record for 0–186mph, at just 13.6 seconds.

2012 Weismann MF3 Weismann produce incredible, hand-built conceptual supercars with completely unique styling. The company logo is a gecko, since these cars stick to the road like that agile lizard. The craftsmanship is staggering, with the wiring loom alone taking four days to assemble, while even the solid brass gecko logo is handmade.

2013 Rolls Royce Wraith Yes, a Rolls Royce in a supercar book. Before you judge, though, examine the statistics, the price and the looks and then think again. 0–60mph in 4.2 seconds for a near-2.5 tonne car... Need I say more?

2005 Ariel Atom 500 With its exo-skeletal frame and weighing in lighter than a pillow, the Atom has always been the track car choice for any serious car fanatic. When Ariel decided to slap a big V8 engine in there, too, it was time to schedule the Apocalypse. Sub-three seconds to 60mph is standard for most Atoms, while the supercharged, more extreme models are becoming the stuff of supercar legend. It is one of those cars that you see on the road and secretly want to own. Even when it is raining and you are trying not to notice the laughing faces of people driving past in boring saloons with roofs.

2006 Caterham 7 Supersport R Lotus built the first '7' in 1957, and that car took 17 seconds to get to 60mph. However, Chapman's original genius with lightweight design has been evolved and seen every '7' since get faster and faster. Caterham acquired the rights to the name in 1973 and have since built some of the world's most stripped-out and crazy sports cars, such as the Supersport R, which, astonishingly, has a similar weight-to-power ratio as a Porsche 911 Turbo S.

2013 Aston Martin V12 Vantage S The Vantage S was the fastest standard Aston ever at the time of its launch. For this reason, the car is known by some as 'the angry Aston'.

2014 Lamborghini Huracán The Huracán is the replacement for the Gallardo, with stunning looks that pick up on the hexagonal theme first adopted in the Aventador. The normally aspirated V10 will ensure the Lamborghini's noise levels are suitably tremendous. Named after a fearless bull from 1879, the Huracán is set to be the new benchmark for this category of smaller supercar.

2014 McLaren 650S The lunatic little brother to McLaren's P1 hypercar, the McLaren 650S is a staggering piece of engineering. Taking the precision for which the marque is known, throwing in the stunning silhouette that apes the P1, complete with McLaren logo signatures in the lights and rear, the 650S is a significant new arrival on the supercar market. Faster than the 12C, and significantly cheaper than the P1, the 650S boasts ridiculous performance figures: using a 3.8-litre, twin-turbo, 641bhp V8, McLaren are somehow able to propel the car to 60mph in just three seconds. And 100mph comes along in only 5.7 seconds. That's what you call a 'rush' hour. Curved LED headlights, massive air-intakes and carbon-fibre detailing all add to the car's presence. Reviews were generally very positive, and even the most seasoned auto journalists were shocked by its performance. There are very few cars on the planet that can compete with the McLaren 650S.

A word about track cars

There is an entire generation of blisteringly fast cars that are most often seen being driven by track-day enthusiasts ripping up tarmac. Worth a book of their own, although they are not conventionally seen as supercars, the performance and handling would certainly put these cars on a par with a large number of the supercars in this book. These include:

Westfield
BAC Mono
Caterham 620R
X Bow
Lotus 340R
Elfin MS8 Streamliner

BELOW ***One of the great modern supercars – the McLaren 650S.***

What about?

Here is a selection of really significant cars that are worthy of further investigation. They might not be game changers, or even the most high-profile cars, of their era, but the following list deserves special mention.

2000 Noble M12
2001 Mosler MT900
2003 Wiesmann GT MF42003 Ascari KZ1 (and **A10** and **KZ1-R**)
2003 Mercedes McLaren SLR 722S
2004 Bristol Fighter
2004 Invicta S1
2005 Ferrari 430
2005 TVR Sagaris
2004 Covini C6W – with six wheels!
2009 Devon GTX
2003 IFR Aspid
2006 Spyker C8 Laviolette
2007 Artega GT
2009 Lotus Evora
2008 Porsche 911 GT2
2008 Mercedes-Benz SL65 Black
2008 Tesla Roadster
2008 Ginetta G50
2009 Veritas RS3
2009 Zenvo ST1
2009 Lotec Sirius
2009 Spyker C8 Aileron
2010 Radical SR3/4
2010 Mercedes-Benz SLR
2010 Edonis
2011 Ginetta F400

GAME CHANGER

Hybrids and the Future of Supercars

ABOVE ***The 918 Spyder prototype – the start of the most advanced and technologically innovative Porsche ever built.***

FOR MY TENTH, AND FINAL, GAME CHANGER, I have highlighted not one, but three cars – the astonishing triumvirate that is the McLaren P1, the Porsche 918 and LaFerrari. Only time will tell if these three rivals really can change the game for supercars in the same way that the Miura, Countach et al did before. The early signs, though, are good.

We have seen how, so often throughout their history, supercar innovations have filtered down into 'normal' road cars – the use of turbos, lightweight materials, ABS, spoilers, etc. – but since the 1990s, an interesting reversal of that dynamic has occurred in terms of so-called 'hybrid technology'. The search for an alternative to dwindling fossil fuel supplies, as well as social pressure to be more green, has led the motor industry to pursue all manner of cleaner and more sustainable new ideas. The most prevalent of these has been the use of hybrid engines, namely those which use both a petrol and an electric power source.

However, this is a technological race that seems to have started from the bottom up, beginning with road cars and only latterly appearing on the supercar scene. Hybrid cars are generally quite expensive compared to standard petrol models; however, several mass-produced hybrid vehicles have already made a notable impact on everyday drivers. This is not actually a new technology – a very early electric vehicle was made in 1839 by Robert Anderson of Aberdeen, and in the earliest days of the motor car, electric vied with petrol to become the chief means of propulsion. Ferdinand Porsche himself made one of the very first viable electric cars. However, by the early years of the 20th century, internal combustion had won the day, and for the next 90 years or so that was to be the norm. Then the pressing crisis of changing climate and decreasing fossil fuel supplies made the world finally wake up to the potential of alternative technologies.

The 1990s was the decade when hybrid technology really started to evolve and find social traction as well as financial investment. However, it was not the supercar that led the way but everyday cars such as the brilliant Toyota Prius and Honda Civic Hybrid, the Honda Insight and Ford Fusion Hybrid.

High-performance cars played a lesser role initially, but there have recently been some striking supercar-like vehicles pushing the alternative energy envelope. In 2011, Fisker produced one of the world's first plug-in hybrid cars, which certainly looked absolutely sensational. Tesla also made people take notice, with their own fully electric sports car, which both looked amazing and was blisteringly quick. These and other, similar, vehicles that followed were pioneering cars and no doubt helped alter public perception of this new technology. The question was: when would supercars take all of this on-board?

It was in the autumn of 2013 that hybrid technology finally exploded on to the supercar scene, with the arrival of three stunning vehicles: the Porsche 918, the McLaren P1 and LaFerrari. The three cars had each been in development for some time, and press and public alike knew about the claimed performance figures. However, until the cars were released and tested, there was always a nagging doubt about what the actual real-world performance of the first true generation of supercar hybrids would be. Another question was whether super-wealthy supercar customers would actually care about fuel consumption. Would they simply prefer the internal combustion engine? Was the hybrid project all just a big waste of money?

Absolutely not. Suffice to say, based at least on the experience of the two examples this author has been lucky enough to ride in, these cars are landmark vehicles. The performance is shatteringly fast, and they are game changers, without a doubt. It would be easy to fill an entire book with the amazing technology found in these three cars, but for the purposes of this

BELOW ***The McLaren P1's part-glass roof opens the cabin up to light and space. Appropriate really, because 'space' is about the only other place that you can go this fast.***

OVERLEAF **The gorgeous McLaren P1.**

ABOVE ***McLaren's flick logo is used on the P1 for the front and rear headlights, bonnet scoops and sides.***

chapter, I will try instead to offer a glimpse of the 'feel' of two of these cars – cars that arguably, represent supercars' greatest leap forward since the Lamborghini Miura.

The McLaren P1 had an enormous heritage to live up to, with its predecessor the F1 regarded by many as the greatest of all the supercars. As I have mentioned, I travelled to the McLaren Technology Centre (MTC) in Woking, England and was lucky to see the P1 being manufactured. While there, I witnessed for myself exactly how McLaren rose to the challenge of creating this new, hybrid supercar. The assembly line at the MTC is an exercise in total precision. Expert technicians in immaculate rubber gloves

McLaren P1
LAUNCHED
2013
POWER
Twin-turbo-charged, 3.8-litre, V8 developing 727bhp then boosted by electric KERS system to 903bhp
ACCELERATION
0–60mph in 2.7 secs
MAXIMUM SPEED
Top speed of 350kph or 217mph (electronically limited)
PRODUCTION RUN
375 manufactured, all of which are already sold
COST
£866,000 ($1.46 million)

crowd around half-built cars that have their engines or wiring loops exposed. A long line of 650S bodies take up most of the huge facility's floorspace, but to the right is a restricted area reserved only for building the P1. As I walk through this area, I pass a stunning all-black P1, hoisted on a ramp, its wing doors opened skywards, engine exposed, looking every bit like Darth Vader on the operating table.

That this latest McLaren would be fastidiously developed and immaculately constructed was a given.

The question was: what would the P1 be like on the road?

I headed out to the McLaren test track, where I was met by the hugely experienced former race driver Chris Goodwin. His insight into the P1 is a valuable spotlight on what an extraordinary car this really is: 'Essentially, what we wanted to do was create the ultimate driver's car. We are selling this car to a whole range of drivers, not just world champions or experts, all of whom are driving in different environments. It's very easy to build a racing car that's going to be driven by professional racing drivers on smooth race tracks. But what about out there, on normal, bumpy roads? So, we had to build a car with a whole different range of characteristics, and the only way we were able to do that was by introducing a lot of technology.

'There is a lot of work and thought involved in developing a supercar that isn't necessarily obvious to the customer. It is not all about raw power and acceleration; you also have to *feel* as if you are a part of the car. Anyone who says a supercar has to be a pig to drive hasn't paid attention to the detail. You can have both: performance and practicality. However, to do that takes immense attention to detail. The brake pedal at low speed has to be progressive, the throttle response, too; we need to refine the aerodynamics, focus on the way we play tunes with the steering, perfect the weight distribution, and so on. The car has to be easy to drive as well as capable on a track, so there are a thousand aspects that we need to pay absolute attention to. All these things have to be evolved in minute detail. The P1 is all about the driver; everything is calibrated to give the maximum drive-ability. That is easy to say but very challenging to create.

'However, I would suggest we have created exactly that in the P1. It is not a nervous car. If you want to race around a track, then all 900-plus bhp will be at your disposal. But, if you want to use it every day and cruise around town, then you absolutely can. This is an intuitive car that responds to what the driver wants it to do.

'With a new supercar, you are only capable of changing the game if you quite literally *change* the game – so, don't build the same type of engines, the same type of suspensions but just a little bit better; that's not going to change the game. You are not moving forward. The game-changing element of the P1 is in a sense the fact that it is greater than the sum of its parts. For example, the hybrid power train: I appreciate that other people are doing that, but ours delivers more punch. There is no weight trade-off; it offers better weight distribution. Then there is the aerodynamics platform [the P1's active aero is F1-derived and unique to the car]; the way the car handles, the braking, the finesse...we have taken dozens of pieces of technology and refined them to a degree of detail that no one else is doing, which is a philosophy we apply in our race programmes. So, yes, I would say that the P1 is greater than the sum of its parts.'

There are a number of eyebrow-raising facts about the car, too – McLaren used no lacquer on the carbon because it saved 1.5kg. The glass used is 1.5 mm thinner to save yet more weight. The rear wing creates so much downforce that if it was not retracted at certain points, it would break the rear suspension. The wheels are military-grade aluminium. The car uses silicone carbide, the hardest substance known to humans, and the chassis weighs less than an average man.

'At this minute, the P1 represents everything we have; there is nothing left in the cupboard. Give us another week and we will have thought of something new, but right now, that car is the pinnacle for us. We believe it is game-changing, yes,' Chris Goodwin concluded.

After our chat, Chris took me on a high-speed lap around the test track. I had intended to transcribe the recording, so I could explain the P1's apocalyptic performance in real time with some clever test-drive review and writing. Unfortunately, though, all you can hear is me laughing and screaming.

ABOVE **The Porsche 918 Spyder can deliver 500lb/ft of torque at just 800rpm. To put that in context, the Ferrari 458 never generates that much torque, regardless of rpm.**

I was also lucky enough to be invited to take a few laps of Silverstone in the Porsche 918 Spyder prototype. It was a crisp autumn day, and a select number of potential customers for this €1 million car sat with me as the Porsche engineers regaled us with the huge amount of research and development that had gone into producing the most expensive Porsche ever built. Then, with suitable fanfare, a silk cover was slid off the graceful new car, which brought an audible gasp from at least two of the uniformly appreciative onlookers.

The Porsche 918 is a very different beast to the McLaren P1, but they are both beasts, make no mistake. The 918 was coming to the party with a racing pedigree hard to beat, but also with the knowledge that the previous Carrera GT supercar had not been universally acclaimed. The 918 looks like a Le Mans-winning racer and can accelerate to 60mph in just 2.6 seconds, on its way to a top speed of 214mph...yet with the hybrid tech on-board, it can do an astonishing 91mpg.

My turn on the track was like spending ten minutes caught in a hurricane. I was expecting ferocious acceleration (which I got), but what made an equally shocking impact was the 918's rear-wheel steering combined with the all-wheel drive, which is so brutally efficient as to be almost violent. The car corners with such grip and severity that it is hard to compute in your brain what is happening at such high speed. Yet, for all this, the Porsche looks very refined, its lines are cleverly designed to hint at Porsche's heritage, with nods to the 911, the Carrera GT, and even a slice of the Boxster. Somehow, every curve is pure Porsche. However, do not be fooled by the beautiful aesthetics – this is a brilliantly savage supercar.

To further consider this new evolution of a Porsche supercar, I spoke to chief engineer and head of the Porsche 918 project, Dr Walliser. The car had a very public gestation, as Dr Walliser explained to me: 'In 2007, we

LEFT ***The Porsche 918 Spyder's 'infotainment' console operates one of the most advanced in-car systems ever produced.***

ABOVE ***With only 918 examples of the car being made, this is a view you are unlikely to see in your rear view mirror very often.***

ABOVE RIGHT ***When Ferdinand Porsche was just 22, he designed and built an electric car, known as the Egger-Lohner C-2 Phaeton – or P1, for short. It had 5bhp and was capable of 22mph, with a battery range of 50 miles. Six forward gears, two in reverse, and four brake levels helped the car win an all-electric car race held in Berlin, Germany in 1899. So I'm guessing he would have quite liked the 918 Spyder prototype.***

discussed a next generation Carrera GT that involved just thinking ahead to define what our next generation of supercar would look like – smaller engine, turbo-charged, definitely lighter, with more drive-ability and so on. Of course, we considered fuel consumption, but it was only a downsizing concept at that point, so no thoughts of hybrid, nor of electrification. By 2009, though, the world had changed and so the idea of a plug-in hybrid had come into the discussion.'

Porsche are one of the most aggressive adaptors of hybrid technology, with their incredible Panamera SE Hybrid already redefining the executive sports car market. However, the 918 was an altogether more challenging proposition. 'A lot of things happened in those two years,' continues Dr Walliser. 'There was a GT3R hybrid coming out, the CO2 restrictions were definitely harder than ever; so, it was a big challenge. Something had to change. Until that point, it was not clear whether supercars could even survive in the future, whether they would get social acceptance. And what about fuel consumption, regulations, homologations and so on? It was unclear whether there would be a next generation of super sports cars at all. Perhaps they would just die: the dinosaurs of the automobile world'.

'So, for us, it was either evolve that new way or not create a supercar at all. A super sports car must be relevant for its time, for the customers, for

the brand, for the technology and for future cars. The Carrera GT did that with its extensive use of carbon fibre and the emphasis on being lightweight. The 959 had four-wheel drive and twin turbo-charging. And, so, the 918 is the introduction of the electrification of the drivetrain.'

Dr Walliser recognises that some customers who can afford up to £1 million ($1.6 million) on a car that they perhaps only drive a few times a year will not necessarily be worried about fuel consumption, but he politely points out that was never really a factor for his team: 'The costs of running such a car compared to the costs of tyres, even, is academic in reality anyway. And if the customer has a nice boat in Monaco, then fuel savings on one car are irrelevant. However, that's not really the focus or the point. We have 918 customers for the car, but we also have maybe 918 million fans and supporters who are looking for the Porsche brand to evolve and lead the way. We must strive to be pioneers.'

And, presumably, the 918 will affect all future Porsches? 'For sure. That has already been fulfilled with the Panamera SE Hybrid. We already have a car that has part of the technology on board, not as extreme as the 918 but that is a plug-in hybrid car already in production. This trickle-down effect *must* be one of the most important reasons behind any decision to make a supercar. You learn so much within the company because engineers have to

Porsche 918
LAUNCHED
2013
POWER
4.6-litre, producing 887bhp
ACCELERATION
0–60mph in 2.6 secs
MAXIMUM SPEED
214mph
PRODUCTION RUN
918 units, all sold out.
COST
£715,000 ($1.2 million)

ABOVE ***The Porsche 918's top-exiting exhausts are a unique and dramatic feature.***

Ferrari LaFerrari

LAUNCHED
2013

POWER
6.3-litre V12 develops 790bhp on its own, boosted to 950bhp with a Hy-Kers system, no turbos

ACCELERATION
0–60mph in sub-3 secs (claimed)

MAXIMUM SPEED
Above 217mph

PRODUCTION RUN
499 manufactured, all of which are already sold

COST
£1,040,000 ($1,754,000)

solve problems for a real car, not just a hypothetical exercise. You have to hand the car over to customers, so you have to invest more for a real street car. This knowledge that you gain for your engineers, suppliers, the team, the management, the whole company is extremely important. Developing a super sports car pushes you to the limit, and I am personally convinced that only by doing that can you really pave the way for truly innovative technology.'

The 918's in-cabin experience endorses what Dr Walliser says, with an amazing central console made from a single piece of curved, touch-sensitive glass crammed with an infotainment system. Porsche wanted the 918 to be a complete car, not just about performance, but also about the in-car experience, the phone system, the navigation and so on.

Dr Walliser is also confident that his car will be a watershed moment in supercar history: 'It is definitely a landmark; the history of super sports cars changed tremendously with the introduction of electrification.' This is not just hyperbole: the 918 was certainly a wake-up call to Porsche's rivals when the new car posted the fastest time ever around the Nürburgring. 'This is real-world feedback on how the car behaves, its drive-ability, aerodynamics, engine power, drive strategy, recuperation, brake pedal feeling; everything is brought down into one single number. That is extremely relevant.' (It's worth noting the Ring record – 6.57 seconds – was achieved with the 918 in automatic and the suspension set to soft.)

'It is very important that for each decade we as manufacturers are able to bring customers the *next* generation of supercars, and by doing that we will gain new fans and new customers, too. A lot of people are interested in the 918 who have never been interested in Porsche before.'

And, as for the personality of Dr Walliser's 918: 'The car is a gentle tiger! If you enter the car and head off in full-electric mode, you have a really nice car, with open-top, enjoyable driving. However, if you drive it hard, the car is so incredibly fast. For me, personally, I am still shocked by the pure output. If you put the accelerator down, it is like hell!'

The P1 and the 918 are competing with Ferrari's own hybrid hypercar, the rather more elusive LaFerrari. The Italian car has the most power, the quickest 0–60mph sprint time and the lightest kerb weight of the three, so once it is widely available to test, the performance reviews will be very interesting. A few teasers suggest it will be brilliantly fast: LaFerrari can get from 45mph to 75mph in fifth gear twice as fast as the Enzo Ferrari. LaFerrari took a more low-key approach to launching, letting the 918 and P1 grab most of the headlines. Only time will tell which car takes the most plaudits.

It really is a battle royale: all three cars can get to 60mph in three seconds or less; 200mph is easily passed at top speed; all three employ radical aerodynamics (with the P1's active aero being the most extreme); all three are easy to drive slowly around town; all three use gearboxes that can shift faster than you can blink your eye. Perhaps most notably – and even cheekily – all three cars use hybrid technology not to just save the planet, but to boost already extraordinary performance figures.

And, finally, all three have undoubtedly generated a watershed moment for supercars and, by definition, cars in general. Have they changed the game? Only time will tell. This is all completely new territory for the supercar world. Rather than signalling the end of the supercar as we know it, maybe these three remarkable hypercars have actually saved the breed forever.

ABOVE ***LaFerrari made a more elusive entrance into the hyper car hybrid market, but its performance figures were simply breathtaking.***

RIGHT ***If you see this in your rear view mirror as well as the image on page 236, then you are either on a racetrack or in a queue for a very, very expensive car park.***

LARK
McLaren
BRIDGESTONE

Conclusion

As I researched and wrote this book, it became increasingly apparent on a number of levels that as well as technical feats and engineering masterpieces, supercars are also highly personal machines. Firstly, the criteria for what defines a supercar alter depending on who you ask. Secondly, we sometimes perceive supercar companies as faceless organisations that run multi-million-pound development programmes in secretive, state-of-the-art factories with staff whom we tend only to see in person at some super-glitzy launch during one of the high-profile car shows around the world each year.

In fact, when you meet the team behind each car, you realise that it is very often a small, boutique group of passionate people with a shared vision making the key decisions. Take that meeting in the airport lounge over the McLaren F1, or the small, personally involved team over at Bugatti HQ in Molsheim, or the 'family' atmosphere at Bentley and so on.

Further to that, the cars themselves excite uniquely personal responses. As this book evolved and I took a metaphorical drive through supercar history, I met and spoke to designers, drivers, owners and the other petrol-heads along the roadside. As I did, it became clear that supercars are an intensely personal experience. A personal relationship. Supercars are personal from the first moment you see them – whether on your bedroom wall as a kid, or in the street – they are personal if you are lucky enough to buy one, or when you drive one, when you read about one or even when you hear one. Eminent neuroscientist Dr Kerry Spackman has worked for Jaguar and McLaren F1 teams and understands what happens in the brain when we see a supercar: 'A petrol-head who is moved by the beauty and power of a supercar has a different reaction to someone with no interest in cars. For the supercar aficionado, the emotional circuits, the limbic system of the brain, fire up and a burst of neurotransmitters is released that is akin to the experience of falling in love.'

This highly subjective element also became apparent when I was trying to pick my tenth game changer with which to complete this book. Some people urged me to include the Jaguar E-Type, due to its revolutionary aerodynamics. Some said the Honda NSX had to be included, as it debuted variable valve timing and threw the Far East into the supercar battle. 'What about the Ariel Atom?' 'You have included the Aston Martin One-77, haven't you?' 'Surely the 288GTO is on your list?'

I tried to field all of these hearty suggestions with a historically minded reply. Maybe, just maybe, the Benz Motorwagen from 1885 is *the* tenth game-changing supercar to include? Fastest car in the world at launch? Turned heads when it drove along the street? Too expensive for the average man? Revolutionary technology? Striking looks? Check to all the above. A game changer? For sure.

In the end, I couldn't find an answer that would satisfy everyone. Then, however, I realised that it is *my* list...and that's what makes supercars so fabulous. The choice can be your own personal indulgence. That's why I chose the three hybrid hypercars as my tenth game changer. You may agree; you may not.

If this book has done anything, I hope it has made you grab a piece of paper and write down your own Top Ten of supercars – a list that will, with any luck, change several times over the course of many friendly arguments before you decide on your final list.

Whether you are a ten-year-old boy or a ten-year-old boy at heart, these supercars are for you.

They changed the supercar game. Therefore they changed *my* supercar game.

The question is, which supercars changed yours?

BUGATTI

Afterword by Dr Wolfgang Schreiber,

President of Bugatti and CEO and Chairman of Bentley

A supercar has to be an emotional experience. There are some very obvious criteria that qualify a car as a supercar, but for me the emotion it excites is perhaps the single-most important factor. Yes, a supercar needs high performance or a technical element that sets it apart from anything else; it is usually made in only a limited production run; a high price is to be expected; the statistics and performance numbers matter; the look has to be striking, too; people look to a certain pedigree of supercar also. All of those things count, but above all, it has to be emotional.

This emotion is not just for the owner to experience. Only a lucky few people buy supercars, but around the world there are millions of fans. For example, there are only about 450 Bugatti Veyrons in the world, and most of them are parked up or garaged, so you can't even see them. Yet Bugatti has more than two million fans on social media. Very young people enjoy supercars, too. They know very well what a supercar is, they know what it takes and they want to know more all the time. Supercars become a part of their life. This is what supercars do.

Great supercars also have a personality of their own: a character. You want to own a car that has a soul. Some supercars take you racing, some are easy to drive, some can do both, but all good supercars have these distinct personalities. Whenever I drive a Bugatti Veyron, it gives me a feeling of changing the fundamentals of physics, because you can't believe what that car can do. I was lucky enough to have the opportunity to work on the Veyron. This means that a part of me is embedded in that car, but its soul and personality still surprise me to this day.

This personality is strongest in the best supercars. You can park a genuine supercar wherever you want in the street without any danger of someone scratching it. People don't damage a real supercar; they just stand back and admire it. They might stroke it, but they don't scratch it.

There is a serious side to this automotive indulgence, of course. Supercar manufacturers are responsible for keeping an eye on the planet, so the need to develop electric cars, find alternative energy sources, plug-in hybrids, all of that has to be a part of the future of supercars. Also, the technology we create with supercars does filter down, which is very important for the wider car industry. That is a given.

However, there is no logical reason behind creating a supercar. Nonetheless, it is human to want to push boundaries, to create, to evolve. That impulse will never go away. We have to keep pushing forward.

When I was a kid, I had posters of some old Bentleys on my bedroom wall, a few V8 muscle cars, the Jaguar E-Type and also a Porsche 911. I used to look at them, and they gave me an emotional, exciting feeling. And when I see a supercar now, as an adult, I get exactly the same feeling. In that sense, nothing has changed for me. You need to still feel like the boy looking at those posters. If I cannot become a boy again when I sit in a supercar, then I cannot do my job properly. At times, yes, you need to be a senior manager or a chief engineer, and there are some very serious elements of my work, but in all of our jobs we need to have moments when we are that boy again, looking at those posters, getting that emotional attachment, that excitement, otherwise you lose something very important. It has to come from the heart – and the petrol-head.

Nobody puts supercars in the scrapyard. You hand these cars down to your kids. These cars stay always in your mind. Even if you don't own a supercar, they live in the minds of people, in books like this one that Martin has written, in culture, in conversation, in life.

Supercars don't die. They live forever.

Dr Wolfgang Schreiber, President of Bugatti and CEO and Chairman of Bentley

Index

Page references in *italics* indicate photographs.

A

AC:
Ace 44
Daytona Coupe 45
Shelby Cobra 44–5, *44*, *45*, 82
Alfa Romeo 80
Carabo 58, *58*, 92, *92*
8C 20, 21
Navajo 87
Tipo 33
Stradale 71, 92
Allard J1 22
Allen, Tim 81
AMG 29, 32, 34, 170, 208
Amian, Dominik 168
Amon, Chris 67
Anderson, Robert 228
Andretti, Mario 99
Ariel Atom 223, 244
Artego GT 225
Artoli, Romano 148, 149
Ascari:
Ecosse 177
KZ1 225
Aston Martin 80, 108
Bulldog 105
DB2 *36*, 37
DB4 22, 68, *68*, 71
DB5 69
DBS 105
Mk II 21
One-77 198–9, *198–9*, 244
Vantage V8 104–5, 140, *140*
Vantage S V12 224
Vanquish 214
Audi 134, 203, 204
Quattro 107, 122, 218
R8 219

B

Bamato, Woolf 'Babe' 210
Bentley Boys, The *17*, 210
Bentley, W. O. 210
Bentley 247
Blower 18, *18–19*, 20, 209
Continental GT Speed 209–11, *211*, 212–13, *212*, *213*
Continental R 211
Mulsanne 211
Benz Motorwagen *14*, 15, 23, 244
Benz, Bertha 15–16
Benz, Carl 15
Bertone design company 61, 92
Birmingham Motor Show 162
Bizzarrini 42, 70
BMW:
M1 101, *101*
Motorsport 154
3-Series 80
Bond, James 98, 99, 100, 104, 110
Bosi 215
Boss 302 Mustang 78
Brabham 153, 156
Brembo 163
Bristol Fighter 225
Broccoli, Cubby 99
Brooklands 29, 34
Brouhot 17
Buick:
Century 75
GSK 78
Bugatti 44, 247
Atlantic 148, *190*, 191
EB110 143, 148–9, *148–9*, 162
Molsheim HQ 243
Royale 148
Type 35 20, 22
Type 43 22
Type 57 20
Type 235 61
Veyron 11, *13*, 49, 82, 125, 161, 168, 188–91, *188–9*, *190–1*, *192–3*, 193, *194–5*, 196, *196*, *197*, 198, 203, 204, 205, 218, 219, 222, *244–5*, *246–7*, 247–8
Bugatti, Ettore 17, 169, 190, 210

C

Callaway, Reeves 80
Callaway C12 80
Caparo T1 219, *219*
Catalina 74
Caterham 7 139, 224
Chapman, Colin 39, 60–1, 99, 100
Chasseloup-Laubat, Gaston de 17
Chevrolet 152
Camaro 78, 79
Chevelle 78, *78*
Corvette 37, *37*, 72, 74, 80
Corvette Stingray 71
Nova SS 79
Chrysler 37, 80, 82, 146
Hemi 75
300 20
Cisitalia 202 21
Citroen 88
SM 102
Cizeta Moroder 174
Cooper, John 39
Coulthard, David 6–9, *7*
Covini C6W 225

D

Da Vinci, Leonardo 170
Daimler-Benz 26
Dare DZ 177
Darracq 17
Dean, James 23
DeLorean, John 109, 110
Dennis, Ron 153, 154
Detroit Motor Show 82

Devon GTX 225
DeLorean 80, 88
  DMC-12 108–10, *108*, *109*
De Tomaso:
  Guara 174
  Pantera 103, *103*
Dodge:
  Challenger 78
  Charger 78
  D-500 75
  Roadrunner 78
  Viper 80, 82–3, *83*
Dome Zero 105
Duesenberg 20, *20*
Dymock, Eric 67

E
Egger-Lohner C-2 Phaeton (P1) 236
Evans, Chris 133

F
Fangio, Juan Manuel 88, 169
Ferrari 8, 100, 196
  125 Sport 22
  166 MM Barchetta 22
  250GTO 23, 42–4, *42*, *43*, 45, 59, 61, 219
  250LM 69
  275GTB 69, 71
  288GTO *106*, 108, 110–13, *111*, *112*, *113*, 114, 130, 134, 162, 168, 219, 244
  308GT/4, 308GTB 58, *84*, 105, *104–5*, 110, 133
  328 63
  348 141, 148
  355 148, 175, *175*
  365 GT4/BB Berlinetta Boxer 87, 133, 141
  365 GTB Daytona 63, 64, 70, 71, *71*, 87, 88, 93, 133
  355GTS 63
  375MM 23
  400GT Superamerica 50, 69, *69*
  430 225
  458 9, 201, 220, 221, 234
  512 103, 133
  550 Maranello 23, 177
  599 113, *176*, 220
  Dino 71, 87, 103, 104
  Enzo 136, 168, 180–1, *181*, *182–3*, 201, 241
  F1 team 169, 180, 181, 184
  F12 Berlinetta 222
  F40 28, 63, 83, 113, 115, 119, 121, 123, 125, *128–9*, 129, 130–1, *130–1*, 132–3, *132–3*, 134, *135*, 136–7, *137*, 147, 152–3, 163, *165*, 168, 170, 180, 184
  F50 143, 163–5, *164*, *165*, 168, 184
  FXX 185, *185*
  LaFerrari 227, 228, 240–1, *240–1*
  Maranello 130, 163, 165
  Modena HQ 39, 42, 130
  Mondial *138*, 139
  Mythos 164
  P4/5 44, *178*, 179
  Prancing Horse (Cavallino Rampante) 42, 108
  Testarossa 44, 63, 113–15, *114*, *115*, *116–17*, 141, 156
Ferrari, Enzo 17, 59, 67, 71, 130, 137, 169, 185, 210
Fiat BV Zagato *36*, 37
Fioravanti, Leonardo 87, 133
First World War, 1914–18 17
Ford 37, 80, 139
  Fusion Hybrid 228
  GT40 64, *66*, *67*, 67–8, 81
  Model T 20
  Mustang 74, 77–8, *77*, 79, *79*
  Sierra 87
Ford, Henry 16, 67
Formula 1 6, 8, 39, 43, 61, 82, 88, 99, 120, 134, 169, 180, 181, 184, 185, 201, 244
Frankfurt Motor Show 52, 121

G
Gandini, Marcello 58, 61, 62, 63, 92, 93, 146, 148, 174
General Motors 80
  Aerovette 80
  CERV IV 80
Geneva Motor Show 63, 87, 92, 110, 169, 198
Ghia 103
Giugiaro, Giorgetto 88, 99, 101, 109
Glickenhaus, James 179
Goodwin, Chris 233
Goodwood Festival of Speed 43, 126, 186, 187, 203, 204, 208
Group B rallying formula 107, 119, 120, 121, 125, 162
GT Championship 42, 83, 184
Gülpen, Robert 207
Gumpert Apollo 218, *218*
Gumpert, Roland 218

H
Hennessy Venom GT 222
Higgins, Steve 61–2, 94, 96, 97
Hoffman, Max 28, 29, 35
Holland, Keith 152
Honda:
  Civic Hybrid 228
  Insight 228
  NSX 147–8, *147*, 200, 244
Howlett, Liam 131

I
IFR Aspid 225
International Concourse d'Elegance Show, 2013 97
Invicta S1 225
Iso Grifo A3C 70

J
Jack Barclay dealership, Mayfair, London *192–3*
Jaguar:
  C-Type 22
  D-Type 22, 35, 40, 163
  E-Type 21, 40–2, *40–1*, 63, 244, 248
  SS100 21
  XJ13 163
  XJ220 143, 162–3
  XJR-15 153, *162–3*, 174
  XK120 22, 40, 42
  XK140 35
Jeantaud 17
Jellinek, Emil 16
Jensen FF 70
Joe Macari Showroom, London 167, 170, 173
John Paul II, Pope 184
Johnson, Lyndon 76

K
Kankkunen, Juha 212

Karidis, Alex 121, 123, 125, 126
Kay, Jay 133
Koenigsegg 200, 203
Agera 187, *187*
CC8S 185–7
CCX 186, 199
CCXR 186, *186*, 199
One:1 187
Kruta, Julius 148

L

Lamborghini 6, 8, 9, 39, 80, 101, 169
Aventador 201–2, *202–3*, 203, 204–5, *204–5*, 206–7, *207*, 208
Countach *10*, 11, 12, 58, 83, *84*, 87, 88, *90–1*, 91, 92–3, *93*, 94, *94*, *95*, 96–7, *96*, *97*, 100, 103, 114, 139, 146, 147, 148, 169, 174, 179
Diablo 81, *142*, 143, *144–5*, 146–7, *146*, 148, 169, 174, 204, 215
Espada 71
Gallardo 206, 207, 215, *216–17*, 224
Huracán 206, *206*, 208, 224
Islero 71
Jalpa 139, *139*
Miura 25, 26, *38*, 39, 56–65, *56–7*, *58–9*, *60*, *61*, *62*, *63*, *64–5*, 70, 71, 85, 87, 92, 93, 94, 103, 146, 147, 148, 168, 174, 179, 209, 232
Murcielago 204, 215
Sesto Elemento 222, *222–3*
Urraco *102*, 103
Lamborghini, Ferruccio 58–9, 60, 61, 63, 96, 215
Lamm, John 156
Lancia Stratos 58, 104, *104*, 148
LCC Rocket 177
Le Mans 20, 22, 26, 35, 40, 54, 67, 70, 83, 143, 151, 160, 174, 180, 193, 210, 218, 234
Levassor, Emile 16
Lexan Windows 136
Lexus LFA 200–1, *200*
Lister Storm 174
Lola 67
T70 coupe 92
Lotus 39, 60, 63, 80, 99, 100, 108, 139, 221, 224
Elan 63, 153
Espirit 99–101, *99*, *100*, 109
Evora 225
Exige 214, *214*

M

Mansell, Nigel 133
Marcos:
1800 71
LM 500 177
Mantis XP 71
Mantual 140
Marussia B2 (and B1) 219
Maserati 102, 148
Bora 88, *89*
Ghibli 70, *70*, 88
Khamsin 58
MC12 *184*
Masler MT900 225
Mason, Nick 42, 43, 133, 219
Matra Murena 139
Matra-Simca Bagheera 105, 139
Max Wedge Mopars 74
McLaren, Bruce 67, 152
McLaren 8
650S 224, *224–5*
F1 9, 81, 122, 143, 150–1, *150–1*, 152–3, *152*, *153*, 154, *154*, *155*, 156–7, *156–7*, *158–9*, 160–1, *161*, 165, 168, 180, 193, 215, 228, 243
M6 152
MP4-12C 221, *221*
P1 227, *228–9*, *230–1*, 232–4, *232*, 241
Technology Centre 152, *152*, 232
McLauchlan, Donovan 99
McQueen, Steve 77
Mercedes McLaren SLR 225
Mercedes World Museum, Surrey 29
Mercedes-Benz:
C111 102
CLK GTR 177
Gullwing 6, 9, 15, 23, 24–35, *24–5*, *26–7*, *28*, *29*, *30–1*, *32*, *33*, *34*, *35*, 74, 179, 209
SL Roadster 35, *35*
SLS AMG 29, 34, *34*
SSK *21*
W196 Grand Prix car 35
Mercedes-Simplex 40bhp 23, *23*
Mercer Raceabout 74
MG SV 215, *215*
Michelotto 134, 136
Mille Miglia 20, 21, 22, 24, 59
Miura, Antonio 62
Monteverdi Hai 105
Morgan Aero 214
Morrison, John 170
Murray, Gordon 148, 153, 154, 156, 157, 160
muscle cars 73–83

N

NASCAR 75, 76
New York Auto Show 28
Nice Race Week, 1901 16
Nissan GTR 219
Noble:
M12 225
M600 201, 220, *220*
Nürburgring 83, 240

O

Okuyama, Ken 180
Oldsmobile 88 75, *76*

P

Pagani 148, 187, 200, 203
Huayra 208, *209*
Zonda *166–7*, 167, 168–9, *168–9*, 170, *171*, 172–3, *172–3*, 208, 209
Pagani, Horacio 169, 170, 172, 173
Panhard 17
Panther
6 104
Solo 141
Paris Auto Show 58, 114, 198, 218
Paris-Dakar Rally 121, 125, 126
Perry Oceanagraphics 100
Peugeot 52, 121
205GTI 107
Piech, Dr Ferdinand 193
Pierce Silver Arrow 21
Pininfarina 71, 87, 111, 139, 164, 179, 180
Pontiac 109
Firebird Coupe 78
GTO 74, *74–5*, 76, 77
Porsche 100
356 22, 49
901 52
911 22, 26, 34, 46–9, *46–7*, *48–9*,

50–1, 52–5, *52*, *53*, *54*, *55*, 63, 87, 98, *98*, 121, 122, *122*, 123, 125, 140, 209, 212, 218, 219, 224, 225, 234, 236, 237, 248
917 92, 193
918 Spyder 226–7, 227, 228, 234, *234–5*, *236–7*, *236*, *237*, *238–9*, 240, 241
959 38, 101, 118–23, *118–19*, *120–1*, *122–3*, *124*, 125, 126–7, *126*, *127*, 130, 147, 152–3, 162
991 *48*, 53
993 54
996 54
Panamera SE Hybrid 236, 237
Porsche, Ferdinand 17, 49, 169, 236
Porsche, Ferry 123, 193
Postlethwaite, Dr Harvey 111
Presley, Elvis 103
Prodigy, The 131, 134
Prost, Alain 6, 133, 163, 164

R
Rambler:
Rebel 74–5
SC 79
Read, Peter 58, 63, 64
Red Flag Law 17
Renault 6, 110
Alpine A310 103
Alpine A610 174, *174*
Alpine GTA 141, *141*, 174
Rolls Royce 210
Wraith 223
Rover V8 engine 140
Royal Automobile Club of Great Britain 16, 57, 58, 65

S
Saleen S7 80–2, *80–1*
Saleen, Elizabeth 82
Saleen, Steve 80, 82
Sayers, Malcolm 40
SC Aero 218
Scaglietti 42
Schreiber, Dr Wolfgang 191, 193, 247–8
Schumacher, Michael 149, 165, 180, 184
Second World War, 1939–45 21, 22, 49
Senna, Ayrton 147, 152
Shelby Mustang GT500 70, 79
Shelby, Carroll 44, 82
Sierra Cosworth 107
Silverstone 234
Spackman, Dr Kerry 244
Spyker C8 Laviolette 225
Stevens, Peter 101, 153, 156, 215
Stutz Bearcat 20, 74
supercars:
prehistory of 14–23
1950s 24–37
1960s 39–71
1970s 85–105
1980s 106–41
1990s 142–77
2000s and Onwards 179–256

T
Targa Florio 20
Tesla 100
Top Gear 186
Toyota 200, 201
OGT 71
Prius 228
Trossi, Count 21
Turin Motor Show 60, 61, 87
TVR:
350 141
Cerbera *176*, 177
Sagaris 225
Tuscan 177

U
Uhlenhaut, Rudolf 26
Ultima GTR 177, *177*

V
Vaccari 215
Vauxhall:
30/98 20
SRV 87
Vector:
W8 105
WX-3 177
Venture:
400GT 175, 177
Atlantique 177
von Koenigsegg, Christian 185–6, 187
VW (Volkswagen) 52, 161, 190–1, 193, 211

W
Walliser, Dr 234, 236, 240, 241
Weismann:
GT MF42003 225
MF3 223
Westfield SEight 177
Winkelmann, Stephen 204

Y
Yamaha 201

Quick Reference Glossary

ABS Antilock Brake System

aero a shortened version of 'aerodynamics' – the study of air moving over objects.

adjustable pedals foot pedals that can be moved closer or further from the driver's seat, to suit the size of the driver.

bhp brake horsepower – a measurement of an engine's power. One horsepower is the power needed to lift 550lb one foot off the ground in one second (or foot/pound per second).

carbon ceramic brakes a very high-performance set of brake discs made from carbon ceramic, which is capable of immense stopping power and remarkable durability.

carbon fibre a lightweight and immensely strong material made from strands of pure carbon that are pulled tight and usually mixed in a plastic resin by heat, vacuum or pressure.

cc cubic centimetre – a unit of volume associated with engine displacement. Each cylinder has a capacity of these units. To work out the engine size in litres, multiply the number of cylinders by this capacity.

chassis the internal structural frame of a car.

clutch a device that connects and disconnects the flow of power between the engine and the transmission, operated by the driver using foot or hand controls. Some cars have automatic clutches.

coupe either coupé or coupe, from the French word couper (to cut). A coupe is a closed, two-door car body of a certain size, with a permanently attached roof.

cylinder the round metal tube in which a car's piston moves up and down.

disc brakes a metal disc around which a brake caliper grasps like a clamp, pressing the disc and slowing it down when the brake pedal is used.

downforce a force pressing down or pulling down on a car, created by the movement of air.

drag also called air resistance, namely the force of air pressing against a car, which will affect its performance. (Drag coefficient is how manufacturers measure this force.) Wind resistance is created as the car punches a hole in the air and from the turbulent air left behind in its wake.

Drag coefficient L/D, or Lift (Downforce) divided by Drag. Wings on cars make the cars much less aero-efficient, but this is a trade-off as they also allow the cars to corner very quickly (due to the downforce/suction generated). Cars with wings tend to have extremely powerful engines that overcome the drag inefficiency.

drum brakes generally found on older cars, this is a small, metal, drum-shaped container with brake shoes within, which are forced against the inside of the metal drum when a brake pedal is pressed.

fuel injection a system that regulates and measures how much fuel to put into an engine.

gears contained within a gear box, this is a set of wheels of different diameters with 'teeth' that mesh together that optimise/control the speed of the engine in relation to the speed of the vehicle.

mid-engine layout a car layout where the engine is in front of the rear axle but behind the driver. This is considered the perfect layout for supercars.

mpg miles per gallon. One gallon = 4.55 litres.

power-to-weight ratio the amount of power in an engine relative to the weight of the car

rear-engine layout an engine layout where the engine is behind or over the rear wheels.

rpm Engine Revolutions Per Minute – namely, how many times the pistons go up and down in the cylinders. For each revolution, one piston is 'firing' the fuel air mix while its neighbour is forcing out the burned 'exhaust' fuel mix or gas.

scissor doors a catch-all term used to describe a car's doors that do not open outwards, but upwards in some form.

spoiler a wing-shaped appendage to a car, often at the rear, that affects how air flows over the vehicle and therefore its performance.

supercharger a mechanical air compressor that forces extra air into an engine, creating bigger explosions and therefore more power.

suspension a system of springs or spring assemblies that supports the weight of the car and provide comfort and/or performance in terms of road holding and cushioning.

throttle foot pedal/driver control regulating the amount of fuel/air mix being forced into the combustion chamber (the cylinders).

torque the torque figure can be converted into horsepower by dividing by 60 (seconds per minute) and a rather more complicated combination of other factors (radians per second and weight). Apparently.

transmission the mechanism that transfers engine power to the wheels and through the gearbox.

turbocharger similar to a supercharger, a turbocharger uses exhaust gases to turn a wheel or fan that forces more air into an engine, increasing power. Some turbochargers can rotate at over 100,000 rpm and glow white-hot!

V engine this is the most common configuration for an internal combustion engine. The cylinders are mounted on the crankcase in two banks, and their angle resembles a 'V'.

V8 a 'V' engine with eight cylinders. The cylinders are mounted on the crankcase in two banks of four.

V10 or V12 a 'V' engine with 10 or 12 cylinders. The cylinders are mounted on the crankcase in two equal banks.

Photo Credits

The publishers wish to thank the following for permission to reproduce photographs. Every effort has been made to trace copyright holders and to obtain their permission for the use of copyright materials. The publishers will gladly receive any information enabling them to rectify an error or omission at the first opportunity.

FRONT MATTER: INTRODUCTION AND AUTHOR'S NOTE
p. 4, Gullwing: Daimler AG, Mercedes-Benz Classic Archives
p. 6, David Coulthard: AMG Mercedes
p. 10, Lamborghini Countach: Alamy
p. 13, Bugatti Veyron: Bugatti Automobiles S.A.S.

A PREHISTORY OF SUPERCARS
p. 14, Benz Motorwagen: Alamy
p. 16, 35bhp Mercedes: Daimler AG, Mercedes-Benz Classic Archives
p. 17, The Bentley Boys: Bentley Motors
p. 18, Bentley Blower: Bentley Motors
p. 20, Duesenberg: Alamy
p. 21, Mercedes-Benz SSK: Alamy
p. 22, Bugatti Type 35: Bugatti Automobiles S.A.S.
p. 23, Mercedes-Simplex: Daimler AG, Mercedes-Benz Classic Archives
pp. 24–5 Mercedes-Benz Gullwing: Daimler AG, Mercedes-Benz Classic Archives
pp. 26–7, Mercedes-Benz Gullwing: Daimler AG, Mercedes-Benz Classic Archives
p. 28, Mercedes-Benz Gullwing: Daimler AG, Mercedes-Benz Classic Archives
p. 29, Mercedes-Benz Gullwing advert: Daimler AG, Mercedes-Benz Classic Archives
pp. 30–1, Mercedes-Benz Gullwing: Daimler AG, Mercedes-Benz Classic Archives
p. 32, Mercedes-Benz Gullwing interior: Daimler AG, Mercedes-Benz Classic Archives
p. 33, Mercedes-Benz Gullwing: Alamy
p. 34, Mercedes SLS AMG and Gullwing: the author
p. 35, Mercedes-Benz SL Roadsters: Alamy

THE 1960S
p. 36 top, Aston Martin DB2: Alamy
p. 36 bottom, Fiat 8V Zagato: Alamy
p. 37, Corvette: Alamy
p. 38, Lamborghini Miura: Corbis
pp. 40–1, Jaguar E-Type: This is from Martin's Jag contact
p. 42, Ferrari 250GTO: the author
p. 43, Ferrari 250GTO: Ian Hunt
p. 44, AC Shelby Cobra interior: Alamy
p. 45, AC Shelby Cobra: Alamy
pp. 46–7, Porsche 911: Porsche AG
p. 48 top, Porsche 911 and 991: Porsche AG
p. 48 bottom, Porsche 911s at Silverstone: the author
pp. 50–1, Porsche 911: Don't recognise this. Can Martin help?
p. 52, Porsche 911: Porsche AG
p. 53, Porsche 911 RSR: Alamy
p. 54, Porsche 917: Alamy
p. 55, Porsche 911 GT2: Alamy
pp. 56–7, Lamborghini Miura: Alamy
p. 58, Maserati Khamsin: Alamy
pp. 59, 60–1 and 63, Lamborghini Miura: Martyn Goddard and the RAC
p. 62, Lamborghini Miura: Alamy
p. 65, Lamborghini Miura: Ian Hunt
p. 66, Ford GT40: Alamy
p. 67, Ford GT40 MKII: Corbis
p. 68, Aston Martin DB4 Superleggera, Peter Read
p. 69, Ferrari Superamerica: Alamy
p. 70, Maserati Ghibli: Alamy
p. 71, Ferrari 365 GTB/4 Daytona Coupe: Peter Read
p. 72, Chevrolet Corvette: Alamy
p. 75, Pontiac GTOs: Alamy
p. 76, Oldsmobile 88: Alamy
p. 77, Ford Mustang fastback: Alamy
p. 78, Chevrolet Chevelle: Alamy
p. 79, Ford Mustang: Alamy
p. 81, Saleen S7: Alamy
p. 83, Dodge Viper: Alamy

THE 1970S
p. 84, Lamborghini Countach and Ferrari 308GTB: Alamy
pp. 86–7, Ferrari 365 GT4BB: Alamy
p. 89, Maserati Bora: Alamy
p. 90, Lamborghini Countach: Alamy
p. 92, Alfa Romeo Carabo: uncredited
p. 93, Lamborghini Countach: Ian Hunt
p. 94, Lamborghini Countach engine: Alamy
p. 95, Lamborghini Countach: Alamy
p. 96, Lamborghini Countach: Alamy
p. 97, Lamborghini Countach: Alamy
p. 98, Porsche 911 Turbo: Porsche AG
p. 99, Lotus Esprit: Alamy
p. 100, Lotus Esprit: Alex Karidis
p. 101, BMW M1: Getty Images
p. 102, Lamborghini Urraco: I don't recognise this
p. 103, De Tomaso Pantera: Alamy
p. 104, Lancia Stratos: Alamy
p. 105, Ferrari 308GTS: Alamy

THE 1980S
p. 106, Ferrari 288GTO: Alamy
p. 108, DeLorean DMC-12: Alamy
p. 109, DeLorean DMC-12: Alamy
p. 110–11, Ferrari 288GTO: Alamy
p. 112, Ferrari 288GTO: Alamy
p. 113, Ferrari 288GTO: Alamy
p. 114, Ferrari Testarossa: Alamy
p. 115, Ferrari Testarossa: Ian Hunt
pp. 116–17, Ferrari Testarossa: Alamy
pp. 118–19, Porsche 959: Alamy
pp. 120–1, Porsche 959: Alamy
p. 122, Porsche 959 engine: This is no longer an engine shot
pp. 122–3, Porsche 959 and Ferrari F40: Alex Karidis
p. 124, Porsche 959: Alamy
p. 126, Porsche 959 Sport: Don't recognise this.
p. 127, Porsche 959: Alamy
pp. 128–9, Ferrari F40: Alamy
pp. 130–1, Ferrari F40: Alamy
p. 131, Ferrari F40: Alamy
pp. 132–3, Ferrari F40: Alamy
p. 135, Ferrari F40: Alamy

p. 137, Ferrari F40: Ian Hunt
p. 138, Ferrari Mondial: Alamy
p. 139, Lamborghini Jalpa: Alamy
p. 140, Aston Martin Vantage Zagato V8: Alamy
p. 141, Renault Alpine GTA Turbo: Alamy

THE 1990S
p. 142, Lamborghini Diablo: Alamy
pp. 144–5: Lamborghini Diablo: Alamy
p. 146, Lamborghini Diablo: Ian Hunt
p. 147, Honda NSX: Alamy
p. 149, Bugatti EB110: Ian Hunt
pp. 150–1, McLaren F1 GTR: Alamy
p. 152, McLaren M6GT: McLaren Automotive
p. 153, McLaren Technology Centre: McLaren Automotive
p. 154, McLaren F1 engine: Alamy
p. 155, McLaren F1: Can't see this image on my copy of proofs
p. 157, McLaren F1: Alamy
pp. 158–9, McLaren F1: Alamy
p. 161, McLaren F1 race: Alamy
pp. 162–3, Jaguar XJR-15: Alamy
p. 164, Ferrari F50: Alamy
p. 165, Ferrari F40 and F50: Peter Read
pp. 166–7, Pagani Zonda: Alamy
pp. 168-9, Pagani Zonda: Alamy
p. 170, Pagani Zonda interior: Doesn't exist in my set of proofs
p. 171, Pagani Zonda: Alamy
p. 172, Pagani Zonda: Alamy
p. 173, Pagani Zonda R: Peter Read
p. 174, Renault Alpine A610: Alamy
p. 175 (both), Ferrari 355: the author
p. 176 (bottom), TVR Cerbera: Ian Hunt
p. 176 (top): Alamy
p. 177, Ultima GTR: Alamy

THE 2000S AND ONWARDS
p. 178, Ferrari P4/5: Alamy
p. 181, Enzo Ferrari: Alamy
pp. 182–3, Enzo Ferrari: Alamy
p. 184, Maserati MC12: Alamy
p. 185, Ferrari FXX: Alamy
p. 186, Koenigsegg CCX: Alamy
p. 187, Koenigsegg Agera: Alamy
pp. 188–9, Bugatti Veyron Super Sport: Nick Dimbleby.
p. 190, Bugatti Atlantic: Bugatti Automobiles S.A.S.
pp. 190–1, Bugatti Vitesse: Dominic Fraser.
pp. 192–3, Bugattis at Jack Barclay dealership: Bugatti Automobiles S.A.S.
pp. 194–5, Bugatti Super Sport: Nick Dimbleby.
p. 196, Bugatti Veyron Nocturne interior: Bugatti Automobiles S.A.S.
p. 197, Bugatti Veyron: Bugatti Automobiles S.A.S.
p. 199, Aston Martin One-77: Ian Hunt
p. 200, Lexus LFA: Alamy
pp. 202–3, Lamborghini Aventador: Automobili Lamborghini SpA
pp. 204–5, Lamborghini Aventador: Automobili Lamborghini SpA
p. 206, Lamborghini Huracán: Automobili Lamborghini SpA
p. 207, Lamborghini Aventador: Alamy
p. 209, Pagani Huayra: Ian Hunt
p. 211, Bentley Continental GT Speed: Bentley Motors
p. 212, Bentley Continental GT Speed interior: Bentley Motors
p. 213, Bentley Continental GT Speed: Bentley Motors
p. 214, Lotus Exige: Alamy
p. 215, MG SV: Car and Bike Photo Libraries www.carphoto.co.uk
pp. 216–7, Lamborghini Gallardo: Alamy
p. 218, Gumpert Apollo: Alamy
p. 219, Caparo T1: Alamy
p. 220, Noble M600: Alamy
p. 221, McLaren MP4-12C: McLaren Automotive
pp. 222–3, Lamborghini Sesto Elemento: Automobili Lamborghini SpA
pp. 224–5, McLaren 650S: McLaren Automotive
pp. 226–7, Porsche 918 Spyder: Porsche AG
pp. 228–9, McLaren P1: McLaren Automotive
pp. 230–1, McLaren P1: McLaren Automotive
p. 232, McLaren P1: McLaren Automotive
pp. 234–5, Porsche 918 Spyder: Porsche AG
p. 235, Porsche 918 Spyder interior: Porsche AG
p. 236, Porsche 918 Spyder: Porsche AG
p. 237, Porsche 918 Spyder: Porsche AG
pp. 238–9, Porsche 918 Spyder: Porsche AG
pp. 240–1, LaFerrari: Alamy
p. 241, LaFerrari: Alamy
pp. 242–3, McLaren F1: Alamy
pp. 244–5, Bugatti Veyron: Alamy
p. 246, Bugatti Veyron: Michael Furman

Author's Acknowledgements

A huge number of people have been incredibly helpful to me in the making of this book, and I am indebted to all of them. I would specifically like to mention the following:

Extra special thanks to DC for his Introduction and to Dr Schreiber for his Afterword.

Many thanks to the following people for their interviews and valuable time: Nick Mason, Dr Walliser, Alex Karidis, John Morrison, Dominik Amian, The Prodigy, Keith Flint, Keeti Palmer and Joe Macari. Many thanks to Liam Howlett for his interview and constant expertise, particularly on all things Porsche.

Peter Read – you have been a huge help, and I am enormously grateful, with special thanks. Also thanks to the Royal Automobile Club, Tom Purves, Ben Cussons, Michael Quinn, David Bagley, Peter Foubister, Guy Nicholls and Jemma Rapson.

The following manufacturers were hugely helpful: Bentley, Lamborghini, McLaren, Mercedes-Benz, Daimler AG and Porsche. Also Steve 'the man's a legend' Higgins, Damien Percheron, Juliet Jarvis and all at JJC, as well as Gerhard Heidbrink, Rob Durrant, Ed Redfern, Silvie Kiefer and Mercedes-Benz Classic.

Special thanks to the McLaren family for their help with photos of the M6GT. Also thanks to Ian Hunt for his amazing photographs, David Kimber and www.carphoto.co.uk, and Geoff Fennell for his painstaking design work.

Big thanks to Hedge, Adam and Luke Matthews for their research and ideas, my wife Kaye Roach, 'Lambo' Joe Yapp, Mario Nichols, Paul Stephens, Mark 'Buzz' Wells, Leigh Naylor, Oliver Smith-Davis and Rob Davis, Simon Holland, Sophie Yamamoto, Dave Clarke and DPC Media, as well as Ferrari S.p.A.

Thanks also to Steve Griggs, Anita Krizsan, Adrian Crowe, Jack Barclays in Mayfair, Lotus, Simon Gerratt, Natalie Jerome, Laura Lees, Manuela Hoehne, Julius Kruta, Emanuela Wilm, Marie-Louise Fritz, Adrian Davies, Wolfgang Glabus, Joanne Hassall, Jeremy Mitchell, Supercar Connect, Victoria Gilbert, Ten Tenths, Chris Craft, Mike Orford, Natalie Chandler, David Delgado, John Manning, Porsche Mayfair, Avril Smith, David Joyce, Porsche Sutton Coldfield, Nick Hine, Porsche Club Great Britain, Chris Seaward, Justine Bowen, Tim Doyle, Doc Brown, Keith Holland, Dr Kerry Spackman, James Bond, Neil Waterman, Martyn Goddard, Paul Burrows, SuperVettura, Alex Wilson, Mr Bun the Baker and Luke Gilbertson.

Finally, extra special thanks to both Caitlin Doyle at Harper Collins and Rory Scarfe for their belief in this project and enormous energy and passion for this book. Both worked many long, hard hours on this book under extreme pressure, and I am sincerely grateful for all that they have done.